Praise for *Taught to Believe the Unbelievable* and Sister Jane Kelly

"*Sister Jane Kelly takes the Church to task in this book. Her criticisms of present practices go far beyond scandals condemning priests' sexual behavior. What she ultimately proposes is a more open and accepting religion, based on spiritual principles. She advocates women as priests, lay priests chosen by their parishioners, married priests, and acceptance of homosexuals. This is a revolutionary book, one that will upset many people. But I also suspect that her vision is prophetic and we will be seeing the Church moving increasingly in these directions in the not-so-distant future.*"

—James Kavanaugh, author of *A Modern Priest Looks at His Outdated Church*

"*Sister Jane Kelly's engaging book gives us a direct glimpse of the current crisis in the Catholic Church from the inside. We see this crisis of credibility in clerical leadership from the perspective of a faithful Catholic nun who gradually realizes the extent of the deception to which she has been subjugated by those in leadership, but also learns to ground herself all the more firmly in the foundational truths of the faith.*"

—Rosemary Radford Ruether, Carpenter Professor of Feminist Theology, Graduate Theological Union, Berkeley, California

"I have learned so much from reading this book. Sister Jane Kelly not only confronts corruption in her church but shines a light for positive change into the darkness. This is an extraordinary woman, with a message that nobody should miss, regardless of their religious affiliations."

—Hal Zina Bennett, Ph.D., author of *Write From the Heart*

"Sister Jane Kelly is a healer. In this book she exercises the courage to identify and make public the addictive behaviors and lies that keep the Church in the Dark Ages. This book's vision, while controversial, gives us all a chance to look more closely at our own lives, seeking deeper self-awareness and greater awareness of our spiritual identity. Perhaps in the process we will all demand more of our religious leaders."

—Philip Kavanaugh, M.D., author of *Magnificent Addiction: Discovering Addiction as Gateway to Healing.*

"Sister Jane Kelly's book reflects the integrity and the courage of Nano Nagle, the foundress of our order. It is written in an easy reading style, addressing issues and challenges in the Church today, and presents the reader with a vision of hope for our Church, the people of God."

—Sister Mary Jane Floyd, P.B.V.M., Catholic Worker House, Redwood City, California

"If you want to get Sister Jane Kelly's Irish up, just mention the men that are running the Catholic Church on the West Coast. You'll get an ear full. And try putting one over on her, and you're treading on dangerous ground. A bishop, now in exile, learned that the hard way."

—Mark R. Day, *The Irish Herald*

Mary H. Clark
41 Emerson Street
Springfield, MA 01118

Taught to Believe the Unbelievable

Taught to Believe the Unbelievable

✦

A New Vision of Hope
for the Catholic Church and Society

Sister Jane Kelly, P.B.V.M.

iUniverse Star
New York Lincoln Shanghai

Taught to Believe the Unbelievable
A New Vision of Hope for the Catholic Church and Society

iUniverse Star
an iUniverse, Inc. imprint

For information address:
iUniverse, Inc.
2021 Pine Lake Road, Suite 100
Lincoln, NE 68512
www.iuniverse.com

ISBN: 0-595-29780-3

Printed in the United States of America

This book is dedicated to
my twin sister Mary Kay Barrow
and her husband James L. Barrow,
who are always there for me…

and to my nephew Sam Hamann and
his partner Scott Daigre,
who are an example to me of what
it means to be in a loving and
committed relationship.

Contents

Acknowledgments

When I look back to the time that I first decided to write a book, I see how incredibly naïve I was regarding the necessary components of having a book published. How grateful I was that my twin sister and her husband Jim Barrow were there from the beginning to lend tremendous support—spiritually, emotionally, financially, and in every other way.

From the inception to the completion of my book, countless people have lent their skills and support.

Thanks to Joan Hermann, who freely offered to edit my book and who has done so for the full two years it has taken me to write it. She spent hours proofreading my manuscript. Without her help, I believe the book would still be in the twilight zone awaiting publication.

Joan put me in touch with Hal Zina Bennett, an editor, publisher, and an agent in his own right. I'm grateful that Hal took the risk of editing a manuscript by a fledgling author.

Because he lived out of town, Hal suggested I ask Jan Allegretti to take over the editing, since she lived in town and would be more accessible. What a gift that Jan and her beautiful Great Dane Savannah came into my life. Jan became not only my editor, but also a dear friend. I am convinced, after working with Jan, that an author is only as good as her or his editor.

I'm indebted to R. S. Gardner, M.D., for suggesting that I write a book and for being there to help me deal with the stress of going public with my story.

…to Mike Geniella, of the *Press Democrat*, and his editor, who had the courage and integrity to put my story in print.

...to Mike's wife Terese, who was there to relay messages back and forth between Mike and myself, and who supported us throughout the ordeal.

...to Don Hoard and his wife Marilyn, who took the time to share with me all that they had experienced for ten years in working to have Reverend Gary Timmons arrested and jailed. Their input was invaluable to me.

...to John and Arleen Keefe, who gave me my first computer and launched me into the world of computers. Both they and their daughter Heidi have supported me over the years.

Grateful thanks to all the members of my family who supported me and encouraged me to write a book.

...to my niece Nancy Brennan and her husband Tim and their children Emma and David.

...to my nephew Michael Hamann and his wife Kathy and their daughter Charley.

...to my nephew Kelly Hamann and his wife Lisa and their children Tracey and Kyle.

...to my nephew Sam Hamann and his partner Scott Daigre, who shared with me and gave me insights into what it means to be a homosexual in today's Church and society.

...to my nephew John Hamann and his wife Robin and their three children Jacqueline, Kevin and Alex.

...to my Godson Tom Segar, his wife Lucinda and their daughter Susan. Tom encouraged me years ago to write a book. When I decided to write, Lucinda, who is an author herself, gave me invaluable hints.

My deepest gratitude goes to the members of my Covenant Faith Community, Sisters Lucia Lodolo, Kathleen Healy, Maryann Healy, Cleta Herold, Marilyn Medau, Kathleen Curtin, Mary Jane Floyd, Ramona Michaels, Katie Burke, and former members Ruth Patrick and Monica Miller, who supported me both by their presence at our monthly gathering and by their continued prayers and support.

Love and thanks to my dear friend Mary Chevalier, who was diagnosed with cancer and told that she had only two to six weeks to live; she accepted it as a woman of faith. It is now eight months later and she continues to say her "Fiat" as did Mary when told by an angel that she was to be the mother of God. "Be it done unto me according to your will."

...to Leslie Loopstra, who took over my programs when I resigned from the parish, and her husband Scott, who installed my new computer and instructed me as to how I could access information from the internet.

...to their children James and Julie, who so delight me.

...to Shannon Phelan and her husband George, with their children Carmen and Vincente, who rescued me from isolation and took me to concerts in the park.

...to Martin Bradley and his wife Debra, who launched me into a whole new ministry to the poor and the homeless of Ukiah.

...to their children Mira, Marjorie and Caleb, who accompanied their parents as they cooked meals at Plowshares, and were on hand on Christmas Eve to set up Santa's workshop with gifts for the poor and the homeless children of the area.

...to all of the parishioners of Saint Mary of the Angels parish as well as the people of the community who have supported me during this time.

...to Mary Jo Hildebrand and her husband Bob, as well as Patricia and Lee Enemark, for their hours of helping me to improve my computer skills.

...to Patricia and Larry Hartly, M.D., who have supported me from the word go.

...to Carol Wells, who took on the job of organizing the volunteers from St. Mary of the Angels parish, as well as taking care of the book-keeping for Plowshares Community Dining Room from the day we opened in November of 1983.

...to Penny and Paul Marchand, whose friendship was always there when I needed it.

...to Susan Crane, who has "walked the talk," and allowed herself to be arrested and imprisoned for her demonstrations against nuclear weapons.

...to all of the people who wrote, phoned or emailed me from across the nation, thanking me for going public.

To name everyone who has been supportive of me would take a volume in itself. In fact, I have come to realize that the most difficult task for an author is writing the acknowledgements. For those I have not listed here, know that you have my heartfelt gratitude.

Prologue

This book is about a "New Vision of Hope for the Roman Catholic Church and Society." The content rises up from the ashes of recent scandals in the Catholic Church, and from my own experience dealing with the misconduct of several priests and bishops in my own diocese. Yet what has happened in the Church perhaps only mirrors a prevailing loss of conscience and caring for humanity that permeates many of the institutions in the larger culture.

For me, the scandals within the Church were not stumbling blocks, but rather stepping stones that took me to a deeper understanding of my faith and gave me an opportunity to question all of the beliefs that I had been taught as a child. Those stepping stones led me through a personal crisis of faith in which I found that many of those beliefs were, after all, unbelievable.

In the fall of 1999 I bumped into a wall of misconduct, denial, secrecy and self-preservation among Church officials. When I failed in my repeated attempts to see that all clerics involved be held accountable, I soon found myself in the epicenter of a whirlwind of deceit and destruction that forced me to question the substance of the faith that had governed my life for fifty years. What I saw happening around me flew in the face of that faith, and didn't fit into any model I knew of the Church that was supposed to sustain it.

I saw that priests in my own diocese had been molesting children and stealing money from the Church.

I saw that Church authorities were not only unwilling to hold those priests accountable, but were also unwilling to remove them from circumstances that provided opportunities to molest and steal again and again and again.

I saw the children who had been molested by these priests growing into troubled young men and women, their lives destroyed by alcohol, drugs, even suicide as they struggled to escape the horrors of the betrayal they had experienced at the hands of those ordained to be Christ's ministers.

I saw that the perpetrators and enablers of the abuse were among the very men I had been taught to trust on blind faith and obey without question, the very men to whom I had turned for most of my life to hear the word of God. And I saw that for fifty years I had taught count- less parishioners—many of them the victims of pedophilic priests—to do the same.

I saw the institution of the Roman Catholic Church, the rock on which I had built my vocation and my life, participating in this devas- tating betrayal of its people, by virtue of its official stance of secrecy and its commitment to preserve its wealth and power regardless of the cost to its followers.

One cannot remain at the epicenter of such betrayal for long with- out soon finding it impossible to trust anyone. I was forced to step out of that place and look with new eyes on all those truths I had accepted on blind faith. For the first time in my life I began to listen to my own conscience. It was as though I had been standing in a house where the windows were all caked with dust, so that no light could shine in. As I began to wipe away the film, a brilliant light poured through and I could peer through the glass to see a beautiful garden outside.

For the first time I could see the truth that lay within my own heart.

This book is the result of that peek through the window. When I began to realize that much of what I had been taught all my life is, in fact, unbelievable, and that the practices of the hierarchy of the Church perpetuate a culture of power and authority with a tenacity that leaves molested children and impoverished parishes in its wake, I could not remain silent. It is silence and blind acceptance of authority that has allowed the Church to continue unimpeded in its self-serving rule over its followers. And it is that same silence and blind acceptance that allows civil leaders to steal the power of the people in a democratic society, and enables corporations to impose their profit-centered policies regardless of the cost to our culture, our environment or our liberty.

It's time for the silence to end. I offer this book as a testament to the truth—the real truth as I have seen it, as I feel it, and as I believe it in my heart and in my conscience. I do so with the prayer that it will open the window of hope for a new vision for the Church and for our society—a vision in which each of us holds our own conscience as the highest authority in our lives.

For fifty years I was taught to believe the unbelievable. I invite you to join me as we embrace a broader vision of truth.

By Way of Introduction...

I think it is important for you, the reader, to know who I am and where I come from, so that you will understand how deeply rooted my life is in the Catholic Church, and to fully appreciate the significance for me of questioning the structure and teachings of the Church.

I was brought into this world on April 8, 1930, just a moment behind my twin sister Kay. We were officially Catholics from the first moments of life—the doctor did not believe that we would live, and so we were baptized at birth. I think it is worthwhile to note that my mother and father were told that delivering two babies could cost my mother her life; they were advised to abort us. I am happy to say that both of my parents were unwavering in their belief that there was no choice: The babies must be delivered. Thankfully, mother and babies all survived.

As we were growing up, my mother attended Mass every single day, and when we reached the age of nine my sister and I were allowed to go with her. The Mass was held at 6:40 a.m., and Mother thought that was too early for us when we were younger. My brother Casey, who was two years older than Kay and I, was an altar boy and served the daily Mass. Sunday Mass was a family event. My father belonged to the Knights of Columbus, a Catholic organization for men, and was an usher at the 9:00 a.m. service, while Mother sang in the choir and my brother served as usual, as an altar boy. This was how we spent our Sunday mornings for years.

In 1941 we moved to San Francisco because World War II had been declared and, as a contingency of the deferment granted him as the father of young children, Dad had to get a job in a war factory. He left his job as a reporter and started working for Bethlehem Steel, which built war ships. Mother had a dream come true when Casey enrolled at

1

Saint Ignatius High School to be taught by Jesuit priests. My sister and I started school at Saint Agnes, which was run by the Sisters of the Presentation of the Blessed Virgin Mary. Little did I guess that a few years later, in 1947, I would enter that Congregation. Not only did I enter, but I remain a Sister of the Presentation to this day. I celebrated my Golden Anniversary in 1997.

My Catholic upbringing was ingrained in every aspect of my life. The sisters at Saint Agnes instilled the teachings of the Church on a daily basis. They taught us the most fundamental principles of our faith, and were also quick to remind us of the more peripheral rules we were expected to follow. I remember a time when I was in the third grade and the teacher was taking us to church to go to confession. All females were to cover their heads when going into the church. I had forgotten to bring a hat that day, so the teacher had me take a Kleenex and put it on my head! I was so embarrassed—but the rule was non-negotiable.

My classmates and I were taught that if we went into the church on All Souls Day and prayed one Hail Mary, one Our Father and a Gloria, we would release a soul from purgatory. One afternoon, on that Holy Day, two girlfriends and I competed to see how many souls we could send to heaven. We followed the rule to the letter, and spent about an hour going in and out of church, saying the three required prayers each time.

As we grew older, the sisters tried their best to keep us chaste. I remember Sister Canice, our high school religion teacher, instructed us to take a telephone book if we were going to sit on a boy's lap. Can you picture me going out on a date with a telephone book under my arm? I lived in San Francisco, so you can imagine the size of that telephone book! Thankfully, I didn't think that was necessary.

Obeying the laws of the Church was an important part of everything we did. One summer day, when I was about to enter the third grade, I was going on a picnic with a family that was not Catholic. My mother packed peanut butter sandwiches for me to take along because it was Friday, which meant I was not allowed to eat meat.

Whenever we moved—which was frequent—our parents invited a priest from our new parish to come and bless our home and dedicate it to the Sacred Heart. He would bless our picture of the Sacred Heart and hang it on the wall. We always had cake and ice cream after the blessing. I used to think that was the real reason we kept asking to have the house blessed!

We said grace before every meal, our evening prayers every night before bed, and tried very hard to obey the priests, the nuns and our parents. We knew that the consequences of disobedience could be severe in the eyes of the Church. There were strict rules about what was and was not a sin, and even about the degree of sinfulness associated with any particular lapse in our behavior. All of the teachings regarding morality were very exact. Each law was either black or white, with no gray in between. When you broke a law it was either a venial sin—punishable by a trip to purgatory if you died before going to confession—or a mortal sin—which could send you straight to hell forever—depending on the gravity of the transgression. An example of this exactness can be seen in the implementation of the seventh commandment, "Thou shall not steal." If you stole $20.00 it was considered a mortal sin, but if you only took $19.95 it was only a venial sin. Imagine, either a detour to purgatory or an eternity in hell, and the difference came down to the price!

If these rules and regulations seemed far-fetched, it didn't matter. There was no room to question, no choice but to accept the teachings and obey the laws as they were handed down. If there were elements of faith that were unexplainable we were told, "It's a mystery." If we felt a law was unjust or irrelevant we were told it was God's law. Who were we to question God?

And yet, if I look very closely I can see where a few small seeds of independent thinking were planted in my young Catholic heart. When I was just two years old, my parents were having a hard time financially. They had fallen behind on their bills, and the utility company had turned off our water and padlocked the shut-off valve. My kind and gentle mother, with three babies to care for, reached the limit of her willingness to obey the authority of others. I'll never forget hearing the story of how my mother picked up an ax and headed out to the water meter. Defiantly, she swung the ax, hacked off the padlock and turned on our water supply.

I should admit, I had some tendency to be a bit unconventional myself. Some of my favorite childhood memories are of long summer afternoons playing with Kay, my best friend Eddie and his sister Geraldine at their house across the street from ours. It sounds ordinary enough except that more often than not, while the other two girls played with dolls up in Geraldine's room, Eddie and I would go up to the loft in the garage and plot what we would do the next day. On one afternoon we smoked a Camel cigarette that Eddie had taken from his father's supply. We got so sick—we never tried that again!

When I entered the convent during my junior year in high school, my indoctrination into the rule and authority of the Church reached a whole new level of intensity. I was taught that I should obey authority without question, and that the will of God would come to me through the will of my Mother Superior. As part of the effort to gain our total submission, steps were taken to strip away our identities as independent individuals. All postulants' names were taken away and each of us was given a name that was some variation of Mary. I was called Miriam. We were also assigned a number that was sewn into our clothing and written on all of our belongings. My number was 220.

When I became a novice, I was to be given a new name, most likely that of a saint, or someone else of the Major Superior's choosing. Each novice was asked to write down a list of three names that we wanted our superior to choose from. My choices were Edward for my father, Eusebia for my favorite Dominican sister or Redemptra, a name for "redemption."

I'll never forget when, attired in my cousin Dorothy's wedding dress and waiting to process into the chapel to become a bride of Christ and receive the habit of a sister, I turned to Mother Gertrude, my Novice Mistress, as she told each of us what our name would be. I couldn't hear her when she told me my name. When the time came in the ceremony when we were called forth to receive our habit, we were called by our new religious name. I was shocked to hear that the name I was to be called was Sister Mary Catherine Labouré—a name I had never heard of!

After the ceremony, my dad asked me how I got the name. I told him I thought they wanted to give me one that was a variation on Kay, after my sister.

The next day I asked Mother Gertrude, "Why did you ask us to list three names that we wished for and then not give me any one of my choices?" It was the first time I questioned authority! Mother told me that Mother Carthagh, our Major Superior, had made the decision and I *was not* to question her selection!

Eventually I learned that I had been given the name Catherine Labouré because a Sister of Charity by the same name had just been elevated to Blessed, which is a step away from being canonized a saint. Later, when I taught grade school, some of my students would call me "Sister Lavatory." My sister companions enjoyed referring to me as "Laughing Cabaret"! Many years afterward, as part of the reforms associated with Vatican II, all religious were encouraged to return to their baptismal names, and I became Jane Kelly once again.

My activities as a novice were carefully scrutinized and controlled by my superiors. We had no access to newspapers, and we were not permitted to visit the library. In fact the only books we were allowed to read were those provided to us, one at a time, by Mother Gertrude. As the Mother of Novices, she gave me the first volume of a three-volume series. It was a thick, red book entitled *Obedience*, by a very stern author named Rodriguez. The texts were ascetic in nature, which means they dealt with the ideology and lifestyle of those persons who practice extreme self-denial or self-mortification for religious reasons. That first book told stories about ascetics who practiced blind obedience. One story told of a monk who planted a dead stick in the ground and watered it every day, simply because his superior told him to do so. Another tale involved a monk who did not eat all of his peas one night at dinner. At the end of the story was an illustration of that monk standing in purgatory, holding a plate that held the peas he had neglected to eat. It was a stern warning against the dire consequences of failing to eat every morsel of food placed on one's plate by those who knew what was best for us.

When I completed that book, I was given the second volume, called *Poverty*. It was filled with stories that were equally stimulating for a healthy young woman. I do remember allowing myself a good laugh over those stories that I knew were outlandish. And I'll admit that I was looking forward to the volume entitled *Chastity*.

The indoctrination of blind, absolute obedience to the authorities in the Church was powerful, and the level of control the Mother House exerted over the sisters affected every area of our lives. Intelligent women though we were, we were not even allowed to write a letter without scrutiny. Any outgoing mail was to be left on the desk of the Mother Superior, unsealed, so that she could read it before sealing it and sending it off. When a sister left the house, she was allowed to carry only enough money for a phone call home.

Whether it was my dutiful submission to authority or my lack thereof, I can't be sure, but whatever the reason, I was made a Mother Superior at the tender age of twenty-nine. I was assigned to Saint Mary Magdalene convent in Los Angeles, and found myself in a position of authority over twelve other sisters, all but two of whom were older than I. That meant they could not so much as turn the TV on or off without my permission!

The Major Superior of our Mother House held regular meetings of all of the superiors. At one of those I said, "I think we have a double standard."

Every head turned. They were stunned.

I said, "Six months ago when I went out I could take only a dime for a phone call. Now I'm a Mother Superior, and I can take enough money to buy lunch at the airport, or buy a book."

"What would you suggest?" asked our Major Superior, who was conducting the meeting.

I replied, "I'll put a petty cash box with seventy-five dollars in it at the end of the corridor, at the foot of the statue of the Blessed Mother. Beside the box I'll put an account book in which each sister can record the amount she takes from the box, and what she uses the money for. When the money is depleted, I'll replenish it."

You would have thought I'd invented the wheel. It was such a simple idea, but all of our sisters had been so well trained not to question the old rules that no one had considered doing things any other way.

I went on to explain that I believed authority should rest not in an individual, but rather in a body of people. I suggested that our order adopt a consensus style of operation. My ideas stimulated a fair amount of controversy and a whole lot more discussion. But soon many things began to change.

Even while I was voicing some "revolutionary" ideas about the rules and regulations governing our secular life, when it came to the fundamental beliefs that were handed down by the Catholic Church I was not as bold. If I had any reservations about the basic tenets of my religion I, for the most part, kept silent and did my best to remember that if I didn't understand, it must be "a mystery." I continued to fulfill my responsibility to teach what I had been taught.

I went on to enjoy a long, rewarding career as an educator and advocate within the communities I served, creating and staffing a "school without walls" in San Francisco; acting as Director of Religious Education at Saint Mary's Church in Ukiah; and founding Plowshares, an advocacy organization for the homeless in Mendocino County.

It wasn't until some forty years later at Saint Mary of the Angels Church in Ukiah, California, that the very foundation of my faith was rocked. When I found myself faced with the undeniable evidence of sexual misconduct by priests who—so I had been told since I was a child—were Christ's representatives on earth, due my complete and unquestioning respect and obedience, I realized that there were some very elemental flaws in the most basic teachings of the Church. When I discovered that even our bishop was willing to turn a blind eye to the atrocities committed by these priests, so that he could protect his own reputation and that of the Church, I began to realize that the vow of obedience I had taken when I became a nun had been made to the Holy Spirit, and *not* to a mortal superior, be it a pope, a bishop or a Major Superior!

I found that the demands of those superiors were at odds with what my own conscience—and, I believe, the Holy Spirit—told me was the correct course of action. I spoke out about the misconduct I saw when my superiors within the Church demanded my silence. As a result, I was relieved of my teaching duties and saw no alternative but to resign from my position at St. Mary's.

◆   ◆   ◆

I share with you this brief history of my life so that you will understand the context in which the events in this book emerged—how I grew up in a very Catholic family and lived in religious life for fifty-three years. You can begin to see how difficult it was for me to confront the hierarchy of this Church that had defined my life for as long as I could remember. I offer that as an indication of how compelling it was for me, knowing that the information about what was going on had to be told, so that the misdeeds that were destroying the lives of children would be stopped. Writing this book has allowed me to share with you how, in the process of learning to listen to my own heart—even when it runs contrary to the orders given to me by my superiors—my basic beliefs regarding the teachings of the Catholic Church were radically changed and my faith deeply challenged.

Even though my roots run deep into the traditions of the Catholic Church, I have come to question seriously the role of priests, bishops and even the pope, along with some of their most fundamental teachings, and I have come to believe that many of the things that I and every other Catholic have been taught are, after all, unbelievable. As a result, I find myself now emerging from a crisis of faith to feel a wonderful sense of freedom. I no longer feel duty-bound to the laws of the Church, laws that I was taught must be obeyed under pain of mortal sin. Instead, I am free to know my own conscience, speak from my truest heart and act according to my own living faith. It is my hope and my prayer that this book will help bring that freedom to other Catholics and to everyone in our society—freedom from the guilt of not obeying human laws when they conflict with one's own conscience, one's own sense of morality.

◆   ◆   ◆

I offer you this book, then,
so that we all may live in a beautiful world of truth...
the truth that comes from the deepest place within our own hearts...
the truth that, as Christ told us, will make us free.

1

The Newspaper Headline That Was Read Across the Nation

Like so many Americans, I get up in the morning, put on my robe, slip into my slippers and venture out to pick up my morning paper. Each of us has a special section of the paper that we turn to first. For some it is the sports page, for others the stock market. For me it is the comics. I find that comics, particularly the political cartoons, offer real insight into what is going on in the world.

However, on January 22, 1999, I don't believe anyone reading the *Press Democrat*, a local paper where I live, got beyond the headline and cover story that morning.

"Catholic Nun Blows the Whistle" was printed in huge letters across the front page. The cover story was about a nun who tried for two years to have Father Jorge Hume Salas, of the Santa Rosa Diocese[1] in California, removed from active ministry as a priest. The article reported how Bishop Patrick Ziemann, the leader of that diocese, as well as Monsignor Tom Keys, the bishop's second in command, had turned a deaf ear to the nun's complaints and refused to respond to her letters. The priests that were on the Personnel Board for the diocese had likewise ignored her.

The priest in question, Father Salas, had been caught stealing from the collections and building fund of St. Mary of the Angels Church.

---

1. A diocese is a geographical district within the Church, under the jurisdiction of a bishop.

But that is not all that he was guilty of. He had also been sexually molesting young men.

Just as the proverbial shot that triggered the American Revolution was heard around the world, so the headline and cover story about the whistle-blowing nun was heard across the nation and even made its way to the Vatican in Rome. And it was the beginning of a revolution in the Santa Rosa Diocese, if not the entire Roman Catholic Church.

I am that nun, the one who blew the whistle. Little did I dream that my action would topple the wall of secrecy that Bishop Ziemann and Monsignor Tom Keys had built to cover the fiscal and sexual misconduct of priests and the mismanagement of diocesan funds. In time it would be discovered that the mismanagement of funds had put the diocese into a fifteen million dollar debt, which soon escalated to thirty million dollars. The toll that the sexual molestation took on the young men involved is, of course, impossible to measure.

Ultimately, my efforts would also lead to the disclosure of the shocking truth about Bishop Ziemann himself. That truth was revealed in three headlines that appeared the following July in the *Press Democrat*. The first headline read, "Bishop Patrick Ziemann Resigns As Bishop of the Santa Rosa Diocese" (July 21, 1999); the second read, "Father Jorge Hume Salas Sues Bishop Ziemann for Two Million Dollars Alleging Sexual Coercion by the Bishop" (July 22, 1999); the third headline read, "Bishop Ziemann Confesses to Consensual Sex with Father Jorge" (July 23, 1999).

Ziemann claimed that the acts were consensual. Nevertheless, the diocesan empire, or at least one of its fiefdoms, was crumbling. But Ziemann had already seen the writing on the wall. In an effort to remove himself from the center of the impending scandal, in April—just three months before the crushing headlines appeared—he had submitted his resignation to the pope. Ironically, when the dust began to clear, it was discovered that there were no funds left in the diocese to settle the lawsuits that were ultimately filed against him.

Needless to say, all of these events were trying for everyone concerned. It had been a heart-wrenching decision to go to the newspaper with my story. That decision came out of a series of events that forced me to reexamine everything I believed about the men who ran the Church and ministered to her people, and even led to a reexamination of the most basic teachings that I had accepted on faith for most of my life. I would like to share with you, the reader, the bridges that I had crossed which brought me to the point where I had no other choice but to go public if I hoped to have Father Jorge removed, and if I hoped to continue to live in service to the Church that I loved.

The first bridge appeared in my path in 1996, when it came to my attention that something was amiss at Saint Mary's Church where I had served for twenty-three years as the parish Sister and the Director of Religious Education. St. Mary's is located in Ukiah, a rural town in northern California, and is a part of the large Santa Rosa diocese run by Bishop Patrick Ziemann.

During my early years at St. Mary's, I was content to enjoy the peaceful routine of teaching and being part of a congregation where the priests were loved and respected, Church authority was accepted without question and scandal was unheard of. But things began to change for good when I started to pick up signs that the unblinking trust in Church officials might be resting on a foundation riddled with cracks. It took several years for all the pieces of the puzzle to fall into place, but one day I found myself with the undeniable and unwelcome knowledge that Jorge Hume Salas had systematically stolen thousands of dollars from the collections that were taken up at each Mass on the weekends. There was also evidence that he had stolen from the Church's building fund.

The first news of trouble came from Russ Libert, a member of the congregation who was in charge of St. Mary's building account. Russ confided in me that he had discovered that money was missing from the fund. He explained that two women in the parish had been sending a forty-dollar donation every month for the past couple of years. They

always sent cash. After a few months of not receiving their usual donation, Russ called the ladies and inquired why they were no longer sending their monthly envelope. They told him that they had sent their
forty dollars each month without fail. The only person at the Church
who could have seen that money was Jorge. What is so heartrending
about this story is that those two women, sisters, one of whom was
blind, lived on a very meager fixed income. Forty dollars was, to them,
a sizable amount of money.

About the same time, I noticed that Jorge had been acquiring a variety of expensive items. He purchased an expensive car with custom
made license plates and custom made seats and upholstery. He bought
two televisions, one for his bedroom and one for his sitting room. He
also added a complete sound system for his CDs. He was wearing
designer clothes.

I went to the pastor, Father Hans Rugyt, and said that Jorge was living far beyond his means. The pastor said, "Jane, we make a good sal-
ary as priests and have little in the way of expenses."

I replied, "Hans, no priest could afford to purchase what Jorge has
in this past year. May I confront him on this?"

Hans said yes, and I confronted Jorge on the monies that he was col-
lecting, as well as his disbursements. When I asked him for a record of
all of his accounts, he said that he turned all of the money over to Pat,
the parish secretary, and gave her the bills to be paid out of that
account.

"Oh," I said, "then Pat will have an account of all your transactions
regarding money."

Jorge paused for a moment, and then told me that he hadn't given
Pat anything for the past year. He asked me, "Why are you doing this
to me?"

I responded that I believe in confronting a person about what I
think they are doing wrong before taking the matter to their superior.
"In this case, Jorge," I said, "I have to go to the bishop." With that, I
stood up to leave the room, but Jorge was right behind me. He reached

over and closed the door, pinning me against the wall. My heart was pounding, and I thought, *Oh, my God, I hope he is not a psychopathic killer!*

He leaned in close to me and shouted, "Why are you out to get me?"

I looked him straight in the eye and said, "Jorge, if you do not put your arm down you will regret it for the rest of your life." I have to admit that I was terrified of what he might do to me. But I breathed a sigh of relief when he dropped his arm and I was able to slip out of the room.

As if this ordeal weren't bad enough, later that week I was told that several months before, a parishioner by the name of Ramon Mendoza, his wife and another couple had made a tape recording in which four young men reported that they had been sexually abused by Jorge. The tape had been hand delivered to Bishop Ziemann, but no one had received a response from the bishop. I was horrified. I scheduled a long meeting with the pastor.

When first confronted with the possibility of Father Salas' wrongdoing, Pastor Rugyt notified Bishop Ziemann who came up to Ukiah to meet with the staff and finance committee of the parish. The Ukiah chief of police, Fred Keplinger, was also present at the meeting. I deliberately did not attend that meeting because I was quite certain that Ziemann would not allow us to prosecute Jorge and would swear everyone there to secrecy about the matter. I wanted a second shot to reverse that decision. Sure enough, all who attended that meeting were placed under a cloak of secrecy by the bishop. What amazed me was that the people who did attend were all very intelligent, and certainly knew that Jorge was guilty, and yet they succumbed to the bishop's order to remain silent and allow Jorge to walk away without ever being made accountable for his crimes. I saw this as a frightening illustration of the power of the Church hierarchy's weapon of secrecy, even in the face of the atrocious misconduct that we were dealing with in this case.

To say the least, I was furious. I wrote to Bishop Ziemann in August of 1998, protesting the fact that Jorge was not held accountable for his actions. I also stated that this delivered a clear message to the priests in the diocese that they need not fear being accountable for any misconduct, because the bishop would take care of it. Furthermore, I pointed out that this hypocrisy would be an obstacle to teaching our children how they should act morally, since the priest was not made to return the money he had stolen from the Church, nor was he held accountable for his sexual misconduct. I went on to say that this action on the part of the bishop illustrated very clearly that he operated under a double standard. Clergy were not held to the sanctions of the law as were the laity. The bishop placed himself and his priests above the law.

Perhaps predictably, but shamefully, my letter of protest went unanswered. It bothered me deeply to think that Jorge was out there stealing and sexually abusing young men. When I read that Jorge had been reassigned to Saint John's parish in Napa, I again wrote the bishop and once again received no response. I also sent copies of the letter to the priests on the Personnel Board of the Santa Rosa Diocese, but only one member, Monsignor James Gaffey, had the courtesy to respond to my letter. This gave me some reassurance, since it indicated that the letters at least had been received.

I resolved to make one more attempt to go through Church officials to have Jorge removed from active ministry. I went to meet Monsignor Tom Keys, the Vicar General of the Santa Rosa Diocese—next to the bishop, he was the highest authority in the diocese. I had Russ Libert go with me. I wanted a third person present when I met with Keys so that I would have a witness. I hoped that this would minimize any controversy that might arise in the future, such as my word being questioned or portions of our discussion conveniently forgotten.

When Russ and I arrived at Saint Rose's rectory in Santa Rosa where Keys lived, he greeted us at the door and ushered Russ and me into a parlor. Before we sat down, I handed Keys a folder with copies of four letters—two letters that I had sent to Ziemann and two that I had received from Monsignor Gaffey. These documents clearly established that my efforts to communicate with the bishop and the personnel board, and their failure to respond, were not my own fabrications.

Tom Keys opened the folder and began to look at the letters. He appeared to be very intent on reading them. At one point he even raised his hand to me, indicating that he did not wish to be interrupted by anything I had to say until he had finished. When he got to Gaffey's letters, he acknowledged the fact that they demonstrated that my letters to the Personnel Board had actually been received.

It was at this point in the meeting that Keys gave an Academy Award performance. He reached over, took my hand and began to thank me profusely for bringing this matter to his attention. I can remember his exact words as though etched in my mind. He said, "Sister Jane, you are the first person who has given me permission to speak about the sexual misconduct of a priest in this diocese. Everyone else asked that the matter be kept confidential. So, I can assure you that I will bring this matter to the attention of the bishop."

At that moment the phone rang and Keys told the caller that he would get to the meeting with the bishop as soon as possible. But it was obvious that he wanted to be sure he had placated us before we left. The monsignor assured us that he would speak to the bishop—not today, since the agenda had already been set for that meeting. However, he stressed that he would address the matter at the earliest possible moment and would get right back to us.

Our meeting, originally scheduled for thirty minutes, had extended to over an hour. Before we left, Russ asked Monsignor Keys, "How do priests commit these sexual acts and then stand at the altar the next morning and celebrate Mass?"

Keys responded, "Unfortunately, that is part of their sickness."

When the meeting came to an end, Keys walked us to the door and once again assured us that he would show the letters to the bishop and get back to us. Russ and I left feeling confident that the monsignor understood the gravity of the situation, and that he would take action and have Father Jorge Hume Salas removed from priestly ministry. How gullible we were. It would be weeks before I discovered that Tom Keys had lied to us.

Because of all the stress this ordeal had caused me, my doctor insisted that I should get away to a place where there would be no way I could be reached by phone. He told me I needed to remove myself from any reminders of all that was happening with Bishop Patrick Ziemann and Jorge. So, in mid-October I took a vacation and traveled to beautiful Victoria, Canada, with my friend, Sister Allyn Ayres, O.P.

We stayed for two weeks at the Royal Scot Inn. It was both royal and very Scottish. The young attendants all wore kilts. They saw to all our needs, and even transported us everywhere we wished to go. They took special delight in Sister Allyn and her faithful companion Matilda, her cane. It was a time that was completely free of stress. There was so much to see—the Butchart Gardens, the British Museum, a variety of quaint sites and the Empress Hotel for high tea. Our inn was located across from the Parliament building and the harbor, which at night were all aglow with lights. I was completely removed from my home environment to a virtual paradise! The gods of weather gave us several days with skies of blue and no rain. The only decisions we had to make were where we would go each day, what we would wear and what we should order from the menu! I think that if I had known what lay ahead of me upon my return home, I would never have left Victoria.

Before going to Canada, I had met with Mike Gienella, a reporter from the *Press Democrat* and a very good friend of mine. I gave him a folder containing copies of the letters that I had given to Tom Keys, and asked Mike to keep them in a safe place. I said, "Mike, I might be asking you to take my story regarding Bishop Ziemann and Reverend Jorge Hume Salas to the press if I don't hear from Tom Keys." I shared with Mike the scenario of my dealings with the bishop regarding Jorge.

I had left my answering service on while I was away, but when I returned two weeks later there was no message from Tom Keys. I waited another week and still no word from him. It suddenly dawned on me that Keys was employing the same method that Ziemann had used, and that was to *ignore Sister Jane and she would eventually go away.*

That would prove to be the biggest mistake that Bishop Ziemann and Monsignor Keys ever made in their lives! Anyone who knows me knows that I *do not* go away until the issue at stake is dealt with and resolved. I don't care how many years it takes. Some time later I was told that one priest had lamented, "Why did the bishop ever mess with that nun?"

Having heard no word from Keys—my last hope to have Jorge removed by going through Church channels—I made the most painful and frightening decision of my life, one that would radically challenge my beliefs and test my faith in the Catholic Church and her teachings. I could no longer live with the knowledge that Jorge was assigned to another parish and would be allowed to continue molesting children and stealing the Church's money. In all good conscience, I had to put a stop to it because I knew that I would have no peace of mind until he was removed.

And so, just after Christmas in 1998, I called Mike and asked if he could come over to my house and bring with him the letters I had left with him. I told him that I would like to discuss the content of those letters, and felt it was important that we meet privately. In a small town like Ukiah, where you are known by many members of the community, no public place affords any chance at privacy.

Mike arrived at about 10:00 a.m. the next day. The picture of the two of us with coffee mugs in hand and a small recorder on the kitchen table is as vivid in my mind today as if it had occurred this morning. We both realized the terrible risk we were taking by going public with this story. Mike and I are both Catholics, attend the only Catholic Church in Ukiah and share the same circle of friends in town. We realized that we would be either condemned or praised for what we were about to do.

Mike asked if I was ready to begin. When I said yes, he reached over and turned on the recorder. And I began to tell my story.

The story was about the bishop of our diocese and a priest who had been assigned to our parish. The story would tell of Father Jorge Hume Salas' fiscal and sexual misconduct and the bishop's attempted cover-up. We were about ten minutes into the interview when Mike leaned over and pressed the off button. We looked at each other and he asked, "Jane, why are we doing this?" After a moment he answered the question for both of us, saying in a very firm voice, "Because it is the right thing to do!"

I so admired Mike at this point. He truly proved himself as a man of integrity who was willing to take a risk for the sake of truth and justice. My father had been a newspaper reporter who possessed the highest integrity, and I told Mike that he was right up there with my dad, whom I admired greatly.

We finished the taping and I gave Mike a list of people who should be interviewed. At the top of the list was Fred Keplinger, who had been Chief of Police at the time that Jorge's misconduct was revealed. The list also included Ramon Mendoza, who had been one of the persons who delivered the audiotape, which contained the story of four young men who had been sexually abused by Jorge, to Bishop Ziemann.

Tape recorder and list of names in his hands, Mike stood up to leave and said that he would clear the story with his editor and get back to me soon. True to his word, Mike called me that afternoon and said that he had gotten the green light from his editor. He would clear his desk and start interviewing the people on the list, including Bishop Ziemann.

I should mention here that I had warned the pastor and staff of St. Mary's parish that I would feel compelled, in good conscience, to go to the press if Ziemann did not take action to have Jorge removed from active ministry. They responded that they understood it was a matter of conscience with me, but hoped it wouldn't come to that. I also contacted my religious coordinator, Sister Lucia Lodolo, and told her that I had decided to go to the press in hopes of getting Jorge dismissed. She in turn alerted the president of our congregation, Sister Adele Hancock, of my decision. Adele called me and asked to have the letters sent to her so that our lawyers could review them to make sure that the congregation would not be sued in the event that I would be guilty of libel. The lawyers, after looking over the letters, assured Adele that there was nothing libelous.

In the meantime, Mike had started interviewing people and working on the article in hopes of getting it published by the coming weekend, but time was running short. We were getting down to the wire and Mike called at around 7:00 one evening to tell me he still needed two people to consent to having their names appear in print, or some critical testimony regarding Jorge's sexual misconduct would have to be left out of the article. He said that one of those people should be Ramon Mendoza, his wife, or one of the others who had been present when the audiotape, made by the young men who had been molested, was delivered to Bishop Ziemann. Mike told me he had spoken with the Mendozas, but they were reluctant to have their names mentioned in the newspaper. They said they would think about it and get back to him with their answer. Mike asked me to call Ramon and urge him to give us permission to use his name.

I began calling Ramon every thirty minutes. The pressure at this point was beginning to mount. I prayed, "Ramon, please answer the phone!"

Finally, at 11:00 p.m., Ramon answered. I pleaded with him to please let Mike use their names in the article. He said, "Sister, I have to talk it over with my wife and I will call you back."

I said, "Ramon, I am getting down on my knees and pray that you say yes!"

I began to pray the rosary that the Mendozas would have the courage to say yes. I got only to the second decade when the phone rang.

"Dear God," I prayed, "Let it be Ramon." It was Mike to say that the Mendozas had called him and agreed to have their names printed in the paper. It was midnight.

"However," Mike said, "I still need the petition that was signed by over a hundred parishioners complaining about Jorge's sexual misconduct."

One of those parishioners, Lucy Luciano, had shown me a copy of the petition months before, and I had told Mike about it when he interviewed me. But I hadn't laid eyes on it since. Once again, I would be in a race against time.

I called Lucy at work the next day to let her know that Mike needed the papers by 5:00 p.m. By the time I tracked her down, it was 3:00 p.m. and she was in a meeting. I waited half an hour and called her back. The woman I spoke with said that Lucy was still in the meeting. I said it was most urgent for me to talk to Lucy, and explained that I needed some papers that Lucy had. The woman was aware of the papers I was talking about, and got Lucy to the phone immediately. It was now going on 4:00, and Mike needed the materials by 5:00 if he hoped to get the article published in Sunday's paper. Finally Lucy got on the phone, only to tell me she didn't know what she had done with the envelope that contained the petition. With that, I heard a voice in the background saying, "Lucy, I found the envelope!"

I called Mike immediately. He was not home, but his wife Terese told me that she would pick up the papers and see that Mike got them. This was not the first time that Terese was the conduit between Mike and me. She supported us all the way.

Having met the deadline, Mike called and said that the article would run in Sunday's paper. I felt my chest begin to tighten.

Sunday came and went but no article appeared. The editor told us that she wanted her lawyers in New York to examine the article to make sure that the paper would not be sued for libel. Within the week, the lawyers approved the article and stated that Mike could use all of the names mentioned in it. Even so, Thursday came and went, as did

Friday, and still no article appeared. Both Mike and I were on pins and needles.

What does a virgin nun do when under stress? She cleans out cupboards and closets. I soon ran out of both, and started weeding the garden. When there were no more weeds, I called Mike and asked, "How much longer do I have to wait for the article to appear in the paper?"

I don't know if it was the result of my sheer tenacity or a miracle, but the article finally appeared on Saturday, January 22, 2000!

It didn't take long for my phone to begin to ring. K.C. Meadows, the editor of our hometown paper, the *Ukiah Daily Journal*, called around 9:00 a.m. and asked if she could interview me regarding the *Press Democrat* story. I agreed to meet her in my office at Saint Mary's school at 11:00 that morning.

I had prepared a press release to be given to anyone in the media who would ask for an interview. I wanted to be quite clear that I did not wish the story to be a sensationalist piece on the fiscal and sexual abuse of priests or bishops.

As soon as we met, I handed Meadows my press release. With that, she started to ask questions and made notes as I talked. After about an hour she thanked me and then got up to leave. When she left I saw my press release lying on the table. I tried to reach her by phone to let her know she had left it behind, but all I got was her voicemail. I never did reach her that day.

Much to my horror, the next morning the front page of the *Ukiah Daily Journal* carried an enlarged picture of Father Jorge with the headline, "Catholic Priest Found Guilty!"

My phone began to ring off the hook. The first call came from Judge King in Willits, a town about eighteen miles north of Ukiah. The judge told me that if I needed any legal services I had only to call him. Tom Johnson, a lawyer in the parish, also phoned and offered his legal assistance. Other telephone calls came from parishioners and from others in the community. Not a single one of them had anything negative to say. In the days that followed I began to get calls from other parts of the country as well, as newspapers across the nation picked up the story. Interestingly enough, no call or letter ever came from the priests or Bishop Ziemann. Their approach was still one of silence.

I soon realized the pressure and stress that comes with "fame." Day after day, the phone rang on and on. Many of the calls came from people who had been molested by a Catholic priest. I finally began to screen all of my calls, because I simply couldn't handle hearing any more stories of the sexual misconduct of priests.

The day after the story first ran in the *Press Democrat*, a glowing editorial appeared. The editor wrote,

Going Public: Secrecy About Priest's Misconduct Harms Catholic Church's Credibility

Countering a bishop's wishes is not something nuns normally do. But to Sister Jane Kelly, there was nothing "normal" about what happened at St. Mary's Church in Ukiah, where she has served for twenty years. So after more than two years of writing letters in vain, protesting what she viewed as a "disgrace," Sister Jane Kelly has gone public.[2]

Words like this, and the loving support of dear friends, helped me keep my strength and quiet my fears during those tumultuous weeks. My good friend Sister Mary Jane Floyd, P.B.V.M., and her faithful hearing dog Missy, came to visit the two weekends that I was anxiously waiting for the article to appear. I had called Mary Jane in tears and asked if she could come and be with me the Sunday that I first thought it would be printed. It was a Tuesday when I called, and she promptly replied, "Jane, I'll come right now."

"No, Mary Jane," I responded. "I'll be fine." She came anyway, and it was just as well she did. Part of my stress was caused by the fact that I

---

2.   Editorial, *Santa Rosa (California) Press Democrat*, 23 January 2000.

had contracted pneumonia and my resistance was at a low point. At a time like this, you realize how much you rely on a friend. Mike had his wife Terese, and I had my friend Mary Jane.

I can now empathize with anyone who is waiting for a jury's verdict. Mike and I were waiting for the repercussions of the article, knowing it would stir up controversy. We had taken my case to the public court and now we awaited the verdict. We knew that we would have to live with the outcome, whatever it might be.

I am pleased to report that we were met with the overwhelming gratitude of many who had read the story. However, I was soon to find that there were other bridges that I would have to cross before these issues of priestly misconduct and their cover-up by bishops would be resolved—bridges that would prove as perilous as the first, if not more so. Those experiences would also prove to have a profound impact on my faith and beliefs as a Catholic.

I would never again accept unquestioned authority.

2

The Clerical Wall Came Tumbling Down

Within two days after news of the misdeeds of Reverend Jorge Hume Salas and Bishop Ziemann broke in the *Press Democrat*, the story was also picked up by the *New York Times*, the *San Francisco Chronicle*, the *Los Angeles Times* and the local *Ukiah Daily Journal*. As articles appeared nationwide I was inundated with calls from reporters and newscasters asking to interview me, as well as letters from people across the country, praising me for my courage.

My decision to go public with the story had been one of the most painful and frightening decisions of my life. It was only after I read the numerous letters to the editor that appeared in the *Press Democrat* in reaction to the cover story, as well as the piles of personal letters and cards that I received, that it came home to me that so many people understood what it meant for me to openly criticize a member of the Church hierarchy.

One of those people was Don Hoard, the father of a boy who had been sexually abused years before by a priest in Humboldt County, California. In a letter that appeared in the *Press Democrat* on January 30, eight days after my story made the front page headlines, Mr. Hoard wrote, "For this lady to do what she's done is mind-boggling. If you don't have a Catholic background, I don't think you can conceive of the amount of courage it took." It was this kind of support and appreciation that sustained me through those trying days.

The sheer volume of newspaper articles and letters that appeared in response to my story made it obvious that my actions had touched many, many people. As I sorted through it all it slowly began to dawn on me that my public statement had resonated deeply and broadly in people across the nation—people who knew, either instinctively or through direct, painful experience, that the power and the authority of the Catholic Church had taken on lives of their own, and that they *did not* always serve the best interest of the Church's followers.

I soon recognized that the incident I had confronted in my own parish was not a unique event. I began to see an ever-widening circle of institutionally condoned misconduct and secrecy that was like a cancer, eating away at the heart of the Church, running contrary to everything Christianity was supposed to represent. The pattern of abuse and cover-up that I had witnessed at St. Mary's Church and in the Santa Rosa diocese were echoed all around the country—in fact, all around the world. There was a solidly built clerical wall of silence that was firmly guarded not only by Bishop Ziemann and Monsignor Keys, but by officials throughout the hierarchy of the Church.

Don Hoard's story was a prime example. When I interviewed Don and his wife in November of 2000, they told me of the morning five years earlier when they read a *Press Democrat* article reporting accusations that Reverend Gary Timmons had molested boys for at least twenty years, from 1969 to 1989. I could see the pain in Don and Marilyn's eyes as they remembered sitting at their kitchen table reading accounts of unthinkable acts perpetrated by this trusted friend and member of the clergy. I could only imagine their horror as they read about those events, and the report that many of them had occurred at Camp St. Michael—the same summer camp that their own son had attended as a young boy. They told me how, as they pored over the newspaper that morning, the phone had rung, and Don and Marilyn had looked at each other, both of them somehow knowing it would be their son. When they heard his voice on the other end of the line they could no longer escape the fact that he had been one of Gary Timmons' victims.

As I listened to this story, I painfully remembered an incident back in 1975 when I was on a retreat that Gary Timmons was directing. During the retreat, Timmons had insisted that he be the only adult in the boys' dormitory. One of the fathers who was a team member told me that he had gone into the dormitory and saw Timmons perched on a bunk looking down on some of the boys, who were chasing each other in the nude.

When I arrived home from that retreat, I went to the pastor and said that I thought Gary Timmons was molesting boys. He said, "Jane, unfortunately we only know of this in the secrecy of the confessional." According to Church law at that time, information told to a priest in the privacy of the confessional could not be repeated under any circumstances. I just remember saying to the pastor, "How can you sleep at night, knowing what Timmons is doing?"

Why I did not do something about this at the time is beyond my recollection. I know that I was acting according to the laws that I had been taught—laws that told me I must remain obediently silent. I like to think that God had other plans for me, and that over the years She opened my heart and my mind and gave me a voice to break the silence, so that nearly thirty years later I could help deal a deathly blow to the wall of secrecy that surrounded the diocese of Santa Rosa.

After our interview, Don sent me home with two boxes full of news articles, books, police reports and depositions, all documenting the molestation of children by priests—not only Gary Timmons, but other priests as well. Over the next five days I examined every one of those documents, stopping only to eat and sleep. During that time I learned that the Catholic clergy that I had respected and obeyed for the past fifty years had a dark and dirty secret. What was even more shocking was that the institution of the Church itself was a participant in the awful deeds, based on a repeated practice of turning a blind eye to reports of abuse by priests.

The newspaper accounts of Gary Timmons' activities and the tacit participation of the Church bordered on the incredible. One of those articles was the same one that Don and Marilyn Hoard had been reading in the *Press Democrat* on that awful morning of November 5, 1995. It began like this:

> Catholic Church authorities had heard that Reverend Gary Timmons was molesting young boys for years, but took no action to keep the priest away from children until 1994, when a lawsuit was imminent.
>
> The lawsuit and a criminal complaint allege Timmons, 55, molested children in his care on the North Coast for 20 years—from 1969 to 1989.[1]

The summer after that article appeared, as the Timmons case went to trial, the local paper carried the unfolding story. On July 10, 1996, the *Press Democrat* reported that the priest would plead guilty to at least one of the charges of sexual abuse, and that the Santa Rosa diocese had already paid $2.5 million dollars in out of court settlements to ten men who claimed to have been molested by Timmons.[2] The next day the paper printed the priest's admission of guilt, quoting his statement that he had "brought scandal to my church" and "betrayed the priesthood."[3] Ten days after his first guilty plea, Timmons resigned from the priesthood and filed a plea of "no contest" to a second charge of molestation.[4]

---

1.   Carol Benfell, "Church Officials Delayed Action Until Lawsuit: Reports on Timmons Went Back to 1976," *Santa Rosa (California) Press Democrat*, 5 November 1995.
2.   James W. Sweeney, "Timmons Plans Guilty Plea: Deal Reached in Pair of Sonoma County Cases," *Santa Rosa(California) Press Democrat*, 10 July 1996.
3.   James W. Sweeney, "Timmons 'Sorry' for Molesting Priest: Admits 2 Charges in Plea Bargain," *Santa Rosa (California) Press Democrat*, 11 July 1996.
4.   James W. Sweeney, "Timmons Resigns From Priesthood," *Santa Rosa (California) Press Democrat*, 20 July 1996.

I was dumbfounded as I began to understand the magnitude of the crimes Gary Timmons had committed, and the scores of children who, I could only imagine, had been devastated by his actions. But when I read about the punishment he received from the court, I was even more stunned. In spite of the fact that fourteen accusations had been filed against him, only two incidents of molestation had actually come to trial before the court. Others were dismissed because too much time had passed since the abuse had occurred. So on September 6, 1996, Gary Timmons was sentenced to just eight years in prison.[5] Because of his "good behavior" while in prison, he ended up serving only four years of that sentence.[6]

Gary Timmons, Jorge Salas, Patrick Ziemann—these men and the horrible acts they committed are just a few of far, far too many similar cases. The incidence of sexual abuse by priests and of cover-up by the Church is enormous. Andrew Greeley, in his forward to the book, *Lead Us Not Into Temptation: Catholic Priests and the Sexual Abuse of Children*, by Jason Berry, calls this "incredible mass of corruption…the greatest scandal in the history of religion in America."[7] According to Berry,

1. Over 400 Catholic priests in North America were caught molesting children between 1982 and 1992.

2. The typical molester abuses scores to hundreds of children.

3. As of 1992 the Church had paid out $400 million in settlements. [*Author's note: The total is expected to reach $1 billion before they are done.*]

---

5. James W. Sweeney, "Timmons Gets 8 Years: One Victim Says Apology 'Too Little, Too Late,'" *Santa Rosa (California) Press Democrat*, 7 September 1996.
6. Bob Klose, "Ex-SR Priest's Prison Release Due," *Santa Rosa (California) Press Democrat*, 27 September 2000.
7. Jason Berry, *Lead Us Not Into Temptation: Catholic Priests and the Sexual Abuse of Children*, (New York: Doubleday, 1992), p. xiii.

4. The Church tried to cover it all up.[8]

It took a lot of convincing before I was able to accept the fact that this sort of abuse is going on in parishes all over the country. Part of me struggled to hold on to the image I'd had all my life that priests are the people we can trust no matter what, and that the Church is a place of refuge for people of all ages all over the world. But as I went on to do more research on the issue, I found too many articles in too many newspapers, too many books and too many police reports, all telling me that something very different was going on. Here are just a few examples:

- *San Francisco, California.* The *San Francisco Chronicle* on August 21, 1994, carried the following story about Monsignor Patrick O'Shea, pastor at St. Cecilia's in the archdiocese of San Francisco:

  > According to a confidential report of the San Francisco Police Department, Monsignor Patrick O'Shea befriended children and sometimes their parents, then used the youngsters for his alleged sexual gratification. At his weekend retreat on Lake Berryessa, in church rectories, even on a trip to Rome to see the pope, the report says, O'Shea spent twenty-two years subjecting children to fondling, oral copulation and anal intercourse. Often the boys were drunk, on alcohol pressed upon them by the priest. Eleven alleged victims—now adults—began to tell their stories about O'Shea to police in February.[9]

  The article goes on to say,

  > San Francisco police inspectors investigating child sex abuse accusations by a powerful Catholic priest were told "take no action" without first clearing it with Chief Tony Ribera or Commander Diarmuid Philpott, a confidential police log shows.[10]

8.   Ibid., p. xix.
9.   *San Francisco Chronicle*, 21 August 1994.
10. Ibid.

- ***Stockton, California.*** In its account of a civil lawsuit against the Catholic Diocese of Stockton, California, the *Modesto Bee* reported on June 17, 1998,

> The Rev. Oliver O'Grady, a Catholic priest, was convicted in 1994 of sexually abusing…two boys from the late 1970s to the early 1990s…. The plaintiffs say the diocese had known since 1976 that O'Grady was a pedophile, but did nothing to stop him from harming children or to remove him from parishes in the diocese…. Further testimony indicated that O'Grady wasn't punished or required to attend counseling sessions after disclosing his problem to high-ranking church officials. O'Grady said he went through a few sessions with another priest but had ear surgery and didn't resume them. Larry Drivon,…representing the plaintiffs, said letters to O'Grady from church officials indicate that the counseling sessions were "arranged not for the purpose of treating O'Grady, but because it's necessary to keep up appearances." Plaintiffs say the church went as far as promoting O'Grady in 1984 to the pastorate of St. Andrew's Catholic Church in San Andreas, where his pattern of abuse continued. "It's nuclear-bomb testimony," said Drivon. "This is the ugliest and most monstrous case I've ever seen. Here's a priest who molests an 11-year-old girl. And 17 years later, this same priest had his hands in the diaper of a 9-month-old baby."[11]

- ***Portland, Oregon.*** On October 10, 2000, an Associated Press release stated,

> The Roman Catholic Church apologized today for one of the largest claims of clergy sexual abuse and settled a lawsuit with 22 men who said they were molested by a priest as far back as 50 years ago…. The plaintiffs charged in their $44 million lawsuit that the Rev. Maurice Grammond enticed them to engage in sexual acts from 1950 to 1974…. Over a period of more than three decades, Grammond served at a home for troubled and abused boys in Portland, for parishes in the coastal town of Seaside and in Oakridge, a

---

11. *The Modesto Bee,* 17 June 1998

logging town in the western foothills of the Cascades…. Doug Ray, now a city councilman in Seaside, has said that from the third or fourth grade until he was a freshman in high school, Grammond subjected him to increasing sexual abuse "as bad as one can imagine, and worse." The lawsuits accused the archdiocese of failure to notify parishioners of Grammond's past molestations of boys, failure to monitor his activities and advise authorities and failure to have other adults accompany Grammond on camping trips and other youth activities."[12]

• **_Dallas, Texas_**. In an article that appeared in the _National Catholic Reporter_ on June 20, 1997, Pamela Schaeffer reported one of the most gruesome stories of all. She tells us,

> Eleven plaintiffs charge that the suspended priest, Rudolph "Rudy" Kos, molested altar boys in three Dallas parishes from 1981 to 1992, some as young as 9 years old…. Plaintiffs in Dallas have described genital massage, oral sex and anal sex—sometimes accompanied by alcohol or drugs. One plaintiff said he had been sexually abused as many as 500 times, up to four times a week beginning when he was 13 and continuing for nine years, according to the _Morning News_, and another said he had been abused at least 350 times. One of the plaintiffs is a man who lived with Kos at his rectory for two years in the mid-1980s under the ruse that the priest had legally adopted him…. One plaintiff testified that Kos had telephoned him regularly while under treatment for pedophilia at a now closed center for priests with sexual disorders run by the Servants of the Paraclete in New Mexico, and that the priest had abused him twice while on leave from the center. One pastor, Fr. Daniel Clayton, testified that his concerns about Kos in 1986 had prompted him to repeatedly confront Kos, and to keep a detailed log of boys' visits to his rectory room at St. Luke's parish. According to the _Morning News_, he said he wrote to Bishop Thomas Tschoepe, head of the diocese at the time, about the prob-

---

12. Joseph B. Frazier, "Apology for Abuse: Oregon Catholic Church Admits Priest Molested Boys," Associated Press, 10 October 2000, posted on ABC-NEWS.com.

lem.... Msgr. Robert Rehkemper, then vicar general, wrote a memo to himself saying Kos' behavior was "just suspicious," but that there was "no evidence" he was an abuser. However, Rehkemper warned Kos that he could be suspended if boys continued to sleep overnight in his rooms.... Testimony has revealed that the diocesan personnel committee was also aware of growing concerns that Kos might be a pedophile. Nevertheless, in 1988, Kos was transferred to St. John's Catholic Church in Ennis and promoted to pastor. There Kos, said to be charming and persuasive, restructured the youth program and, according to testimony, discouraged both girls and parents from becoming involved.[13]

The article documents the unwillingness of Church officials to protect children if it means exposing the crimes of one of their own, when the reporter tells us,

Fr. Robert Williams, assigned to St. John's as associate pastor, said he had been alarmed from his first day at the parish. According to the *Morning News*, Williams testified that Kos had lured boys to his room with candy, movies and video games. Williams said he had repeatedly confronted Kos about his behavior and had met several times with Rehkemper. According to news accounts, Williams also wrote a 12-page letter to Bishop Charles Grahmann, Tschoepe's successor in 1990, telling him, among other things, that Kos would hug young boys by rubbing them against himself "almost like they were a towel in which he was drying himself." In August 1992, Williams asked to meet personally with Grahmann, who told him the diocese was unable to take any action against Kos because psychiatric reports had cleared him. Later in 1992, when the first youth came forward with a complaint, and with threats of a lawsuit growing, Kos was removed from St. John's and sent to the treatment center in New Mexico. Only then did diocesan officials notify civil authorities of the alleged abuse. State law requires immediate reporting when child abuse is suspected. Parishioners

---

13.   Pamela Schaeffer, "11 allege a conspiracy in Dallas sex abuse trial," *National Catholic Reporter*, 20 June 1997.

were told that Kos was leaving voluntarily to seek treatment for stress.[14]

In a follow-up article on August 15 of that year, Ms. Schaeffer describes

the trial's most macabre moment: When Nancy Lemberger testified that Kos had accepted her family's invitation to deliver the homily at their son's funeral, not suspecting then what she (and jurors) are convinced of now: that sexual abuse by Kos had left their gifted son, Jay, so troubled and confused that at age 21 he fatally shot himself in a Denver park.[15]

- **Ferns, Ireland.** Priests who molest children and bishops who look the other way are not unique to the United States. With a shocking example of how determined a Church official can be to ignore the pleas of young victims, the *Irish Times* ran this story on March 19, 1999:

The Bishop of Ferns, Dr Brendan Comiskey, was told a number of times in the 1980s and in 1990 that Father Sean Fortune was sexually abusing young boys. The priest, who faced 29 sexual abuse charges, committed suicide last week. Four separate complaints were made to the bishop about the abuse, but the priest was allowed to remain in contact with young people. *The Irish Times* has learned that Dr Comiskey received the first complaint shortly after his arrival in the Diocese of Ferns in 1984. It was made by the parent of a boy who had been abused by Father Fortune. The boy was a member of a Scout group in St Peter's College in Wexford in which Father Fortune was involved. His father raised the abuse with the bishop on a number of occasions. In December 1986 a Waterford boy met Dr Comiskey and told him the story of his abuse. Two years later Mr Paul Molloy, who was then 17, made a

---

14. Ibid.
15. Pamela Schaeffer, "Reporter's Trial Notes," *National Catholic Reporter*, 15 August 1997.

complaint to Dr Comiskey about being sexually abused by Father Fortune in the south Wexford parish of Fethard-On-Sea. He was brought to All Hallows in Dublin and questioned by another priest. In 1990 the father of another boy who had been abused while the priest was in Fethard-On-Sea complained to the bishop.... The first complaint by the Wexford boy scout's father was made to the late Dr Donal Herlihy, Dr Comiskey's predecessor. He informed Dr Comiskey. Soon after Dr Comiskey arrived in the diocese in 1984 the father told him about Father Fortune's sexual assault of his son. In 1986 a Waterford boy told a local priest that Father Fortune had buggered him. He then met Dr Comiskey in Waterford and relayed his story. This incident was included with the eight others in the Garda file on the case. However, the boy was 17 when the abuse occurred and the DPP ruled he was above the age of consent. Dr Comiskey reported this incident to gardaí eight years later, when they had begun to investigate Father Fortune. The father of another young boy from Fethard-on-Sea made a complaint in 1990 to one of Father Fortune's successors in the parish. A few days later the priest told the man the bishop's office had been informed. An address of a counselling centre in Cork was offered.[16]

The articles I uncovered back in 2000 shocked me, as I began to understand how widespread the problem really was. The rest of the country shared my horror when an article appeared in *The Boston Globe* nearly two years later, detailing a nightmare that spanned more than three decades. It involved an appalling history of sexual molestation by one priest and the actions of Church officials who continued to put children in his care. A tidal wave of similar stories made the news around the country, as scores of Catholics came forward with accusations of abuse by their priests. Here are some excerpts from the article that first broke the scandal that turned the Catholic community on end:

---

16. Alison O'Connor, "Bishop was told repeatedly about priest's sex abuse," *The Irish Times*, 19 March 1999.

• **Boston, Massachusetts.** *The Boston Globe* reported that not only had more than 130 people come forward with claims of abuse at the hands of Father John J. Geoghan, but it was clear that Cardinal Bernard F. Law had transferred him from one parish to another, even after repeated accusations and rounds of treatment for molesting boys.[17] The *Globe* reported the following history of abuse:

> There is no dispute that Geoghan abused children while he was at Blessed Sacrament in Saugus after his 1962 ordination. The archdiocese has recently settled claims on accusations that he did, and the church records obtained by the Globe note that Geoghan in 1995 admitted molesting four boys from the same family then. The unresolved issue in the remaining suits is whether church officials knew of the abuse at the time.
>
> Geoghan's second assignment—in 1966 to St. Bernard's in Concord—ended after seven months, according to a detailed chronology of Geoghan's service prepared by the church which does not explain why the assignment was so abbreviated....
>
> Pending lawsuits include accusations that Geoghan again abused young boys from several families in his next parish, St. Paul's in Hingham, between 1967 and 1974. One...complaint to church officials coincides with the time frame when Geoghan received in-patient treatment for sex abuse at the Seton Institute in Baltimore.... During his assignment in Hingham, Geoghan... [befriended] Joanne Mueller, a single mother of four boys who lived in Melrose. There too, according to depositions, the priest became a regular visitor, a spiritual counselor to Mueller and a helpmate to her boys, who were between 5 and 12.... Mueller...learned that Geoghan, while purporting to be taking them out for ice cream, helping them with their baths, and reading them bedtime stories, had been raping them orally and anally. Also, Mueller said, Geoghan was insisting they tell no one. "We couldn't tell you because Father said it was a confessional," she said one of her sons told her....

---

17. Michael Rezendes, "Church allowed abuse by priest for years," *Boston Globe*, 6 January 2002.

If Mueller had unwittingly facilitated Geoghan's access to the children in her home in Melrose, the same role was played by Maryetta Dussourd at the priest's next stop: St. Andrew's, in the Forest Hills section of Jamaica Plain, where he served from 1974 to 1980. Dussourd was rearing her own four children—three boys and a girl—as well as her niece's four boys…. She hoped there was a priest the children could look up to…. Geoghan, she recalled bitterly, was eager to help. Before long, he was visiting her apartment almost every evening—for nearly two years. He routinely took the seven boys out for ice cream and put them to sleep at night.

But all that time, Geoghan regularly molested the seven boys in their bedrooms, Dussourd said. In some cases, he performed oral sex on them, according to court documents. Other times, he fondled their genitals or forced them to fondle his—occasionally as he prayed…. Dussourd discovered what was happening [and] complained to the Rev. John E. Thomas, the pastor of St. Thomas Aquinas, a nearby parish…. Thomas confronted Geoghan with the allegations, and was taken aback when Geoghan casually admitted they were accurate. "He said, 'Yes, that's all true,'" the official recalled. It was as if Geoghan had been asked "if he preferred chocolate or vanilla ice cream."…The Rev. Francis H. Delaney, who was Geoghan's pastor at St. Andrew's, said in an interview that church officials never told him why Geoghan disappeared from the parish….

Geoghan spent the following year on sick leave, under treatment for his compulsion…. In February 1981, he was sent to his fifth parish, St. Brendan's. Almost immediately, Geoghan was working with First Communicants, befriending young children and their parents, even taking some boys to his family's summer home in Scituate, where—parents say they later discovered—he sexually abused the youths.

Geoghan's free rein was made possible because the archdiocese said nothing to [Rev. James H.] Lane, Brendan's pastor, about Geoghan's history…. After two more years and more allegations of sexual abuse, Geoghan's tenure at St. Brendan's came to an abrupt end in 1984, when Lane heard complaints that Geoghan had molested children in the parish….

Despite his record, [in 1984] Geoghan was assigned to St. Julia's [in Weston]. And in his first two years, he was in charge of altar boys, religious education for public school youngsters and a youth group.... In 1989, he was forced to go on sick leave after more complaints of sexual abuse, and spent months in two institutions that treat sexually abusive priests. Even so, the archdiocese returned him to St. Julia's, where Geoghan continued to abuse children for another three years.... Civil and criminal allegations...suggest that he allegedly abused at least 30 more boys after [Cardinal] Law sent him to Weston in 1984—both before and after the half year's sick leave in 1989....

Law allowed Geoghan to stay in Weston for more than eight years before removing him from parish duty in 1993. But even that decision to recast Geoghan as a functionary at a home for retired priests did not prevent him from seeking out and molesting children, according to the multiple civil suits and criminal charges filed against the 66-year-old Geoghan.

Finally, in 1998, the church "defrocked" Geoghan, removing him from the priesthood.[18]

With the Church's role in perpetuating the abuse looming even larger than the acts themselves, the *Boston Globe* reporters asked, "Why did it take a succession of three cardinals and many bishops thirty-four years to place children out of Geoghan's reach?"[19]

The church's likely legal defense...will be that doctors deemed Geoghan rehabilitated. Church records obtained by the Globe note that Geoghan was indeed medically cleared for the St. Julia's assignment—but not until he had been at the parish for a month. In 1984, there were still some clinicians who believed child molesters could be cured. But other specialists had long since warned Catholic bishops of the high risk that priests who had abused children would become repeat offenders. What's more, specialists in child sexual abuse and attorneys who have represented victims said, it ought to have been apparent to the archdiocese by 1984 that

---

18. Ibid.
19. Ibid.

someone with Geoghan's record of habitual sexual abuse should not have been returned to a parish.[20]

To what lengths did officials go to avoid taking responsibility for their and Geoghan's actions, and acting on behalf of the children? It appears that in at least one case they went so far as to use coercion to deter a witness from testifying. As the *Globe* reported,

A former priest, Anthony Benzevich, has said he alerted church higher-ups that Geoghan frequently took young boys to his rectory bedroom. In news reports after accusations against Geoghan surfaced publicly, Benzevich was also quoted as saying church officials threatened to reassign him as a missionary in South America for telling them about Geoghan. Benzevich told his story to Mitchell Garabedian, who represents nearly all of the plaintiffs in the civil suits against Geoghan and church officials, according to an affidavit Garabedian filed.

But court records reviewed by the Globe show that when Benzevich appeared in Garabedian's office for a pre-trial deposition in October 2000, he was represented by Wilson Rogers III—the son of Law's principal attorney. Then, under oath, Benzevich changed his story. He said he was not certain that Geoghan had had boys in his room. And he said he could not recall notifying superiors about Geoghan's behavior with children.

In a recent interview with the Globe, Benzevich said he does indeed remember Geoghan taking boys to his room. He said Geoghan often sought to wrestle with young boys—and liked to dress them in priest's attire. But he repeated his sworn assertion that he does not recall notifying his superiors.

Before his deposition, Benzevich said, Wilson Rogers III approached him, told him the church was trying to protect him from being named as a defendant, and offered to represent him. His earlier statements to reporters, Benzevich said, had been misconstrued. [21]

---

20. Ibid.
21. Ibid.

Between January and August 2002, the Church was rocked when similar stories of abuse appeared across the country, and the scope of the problem finally began to emerge. Day after day, week after week, newspapers and broadcast media broke stories about one priest after another who had been accused of molesting a child, and one bishop after another came under scrutiny for not acting on prior knowledge of the priest's crimes. By October 2002, the number of accusations against John Geoghan alone hovered near 150, and speculation about criminal charges against Cardinal Bernard Law continued, as he and other members of the Church hierarchy were subpoenaed by a grand jury.[22] Eventually, fifty-eight priests and the lay community called for Law's resignation, and on December 13, 2002, he complied.[23] Meanwhile, as accusations flooded in all around the country, experts estimated that "the total cost of lawsuits, settlements, lawyers' fees, psychological counseling for abusive priests and their victims, and other attendant costs over the past fifteen years run as high as $1 billion."[24]

I could go on and on, and fill a dozen books with stories like these, about how this sickness shows up all over the country, even around the world. But as bad as it is, I believe the revelations that have gotten so much media attention are just the tip of the iceberg. One area that has not yet been exposed to public scrutiny is that, amazingly, the sexual misconduct of priests is apparently not limited to abuse of children. In the spring of 2001, an article in the *New York Times* reported on confidential Church documents that indicate priests in several different countries had sexually abused nuns, and that—should we be surprised?—Church officials had failed to take action against the offending priests. According to the article, the documents suggest that this

22. Walter V. Robinson, "Grand jury is said to call Law: Subpoenas for clerics in probe of abuse," *Boston Globe*, 12 December 2002.
23. Michael Paulson and Charles M. Sennott, "Cardinal Law Resigns: Pope Names Administrator for Archdiocese," *Boston Globe*, 13 December 2002.
24. Charles M. Sennott, "Money concerns said not utmost: Drain on Rome called no issue," *Boston Globe*, 22 April 2002.

sort of abuse occurs all over the world, but is particularly common in Africa. Incredibly, in that country, priests are accused of turning to nuns to avoid being infected by the widespread AIDS virus.[25] What may be even more horrifying, in a related story the *National Catholic Reporter* tells us that "in a few extreme instances, according to the documentation, priests have impregnated nuns and then encouraged them to have abortions"![26]

During those months after the *Press Democrat* first carried my story about Bishop Zieman, I committed myself to learning as much as I could about how widespread the problem really was. After reading story after story after story of sexually abusive clergymen, and of how the Church turned its back on their victims for the sake of protecting the abusers and maintaining its own righteous image, I was forced to listen to what my own heart was trying to tell me. It was only after I was submerged in the murky waters of the Church's cover-up of priestly sexual misconduct that I began to see how thoroughly I had been indoctrinated to regard priests, bishops, cardinals and, of course, the pope as beyond reproach. I came to realize that following one's own conscience was not approved of by the Church's hierarchy, who demanded blind obedience no matter what. Slowly it began to dawn on me that this male, clerical hierarchy was not only wrong, but in many cases sinful.

I spent many long hours and sleepless nights trying to come to terms with the mountain of facts that did not support the faith that I had always placed in the Church as an institution, and that clearly demonstrated wrongdoing by priests whom I was taught to respect and obey without question. Given these astonishing facts, I have come to the

---

25.   Chris Hedges, "Documents Allege Abuse of Nuns by Priests," *New York Times*, 21 March 2001, late edition.
26.   John L. Allen Jr. and Pamela Schaeffer, "Reports of abuse: AIDS exacerbates sexual exploitation of nuns, reports allege," *National Catholic Reporter*, 16 March 2001.

realization that we must bring down the walls of secrecy that the male hierarchy has erected to cover up the sexual misconduct of its prelates, for it is those very walls of secrecy that make it possible for the atrocities to go on.

So how is it that officials can turn a blind eye to these events again and again? What is it about the culture of the institution of the Church that, like a dysfunctional family, enables this sort of behavior?

First, as we have seen, it is possible because the Church makes liberal use of its deadliest weapon—*silence*. Second, the only reason that priests are able to get away with their sexual and fiscal misconduct for years on end without being held accountable is because the hierarchy refuses to correct the situation. There is a willingness among many officials to look the other way, mostly because they believe that the good reputation of the Church is more important than the well-being of its children. Finally, followers of the Church are taught to accept the authority of the institution and its clerics, and obey its laws without question. As a result, it often requires a mountain of evidence for them—just like it did for me—to begin to recognize the truth.

But the evidence is mounting, and it gives me hope that things are beginning to change, so that the Catholic Church's clerical wall of silence will at last come tumbling down. I believe the resignation of Cardinal Law will ultimately have a domino effect in which more and more dioceses across the nation demand accountability of their bishops. No longer will the hierarchy be able to erect walls of secrecy around fiscal and sexual misconduct. In fact, in my opinion, those leaders who aided and abetted priests who committed the worst crime known to man—the molestation of children—should be arrested, tried and, if found guilty, sent to prison. Anything less is a travesty of justice.

Church leaders are not above the law. Pedophilic priests have a sickness that cannot be cured, although the priests themselves can and must be controlled. But the true crime, in my mind, was committed by the bishops who shuffled those priests around from parish to parish, from child to child, for years. In the aftermath of the revelations in

Boston, bishops across the United States have talked of a zero tolerance policy for priests who molest children, but sadly they have failed to declare a zero tolerance for prelates who allow the molestation to go unchecked.

It's important to note here that, while these issues are the fruits of the indoctrination of silence and blind acceptance practiced by the Catholic Church, they are also, without question, issues facing our society as a whole. The lessons we will learn from a thorough examination of the crisis in the Church today, and the solutions that give us hope for a better future, will serve us well as we embark on an era of new freedom, responsibility and accountability, *regardless of our religious affiliation.*

All of these issues will be discussed at length in later chapters. For now, suffice it to say that I challenge all of us to become agents of change. We need to continue to work to break down the wall of silence and bring the hierarchy of the Church—as well as leaders of our society—to moral and civil accountability.

Let's keep them in our prayers, as well!

3

The Roman Catholic Church: A Multinational Corporation

Most people aren't aware of it, but technically the Catholic Church is a corporation, structured much like a multinational conglomerate with subsidiary corporations spread all across the globe. The Vatican is, you might say, corporate headquarters and is legally incorporated as a non-profit organization. Each diocese is also incorporated and operates as a branch of the parent company.

What even fewer people realize is that the Church in many ways conducts its affairs according to values based on self-preservation and profit, much like the unethical, immoral secular corporations that have come under public scrutiny in recent years. Of course, not all multinational corporations are unethical—and we must emphasize that certainly not all priests are unethical. The vast majority are beautiful, loving men dedicated to a life of service to the spiritual needs of the people in their communities. The problem is that I, along with the vast majority of Catholics, for most of my life assumed that *all* priests, bishops, cardinals and other members of the Church hierarchy held the spiritual needs of the people as their first priority.

I'm sorry to report that I've discovered I was wrong. As a result of my struggle to see the Church deal responsibly with the misconduct of its priests, my eyes were opened to the reality that this organization that is so trusted and beloved by people all over the world bears much too strong a resemblance to a greedy, uncaring corporate conglomerate.

The first time it occurred to me that the Roman Catholic Church operates like a multination corporation was in the year 2000, when my trust had already been badly shaken by the immorality and deception I witnessed in events surrounding Father Jorge Hume Salas and Bishop Patrick Ziemann. I had learned firsthand about this habit of putting the reputation of the Church ahead of the interests of its people when I saw the bishop turn a deaf ear to my efforts to report the misconduct of Father Salas, and to the reports of the young men from my parish whom Salas had molested. Not only did Bishop Ziemann refuse to take action, but when his superiors discovered his involvement in the cover-up—as well as his own illicit fiscal and sexual activities—they ushered him off to a rural parish in Arizona where he could continue ministering to the people! Church officials never demanded—or offered—accountability for his mismanagement of diocesan funds or for his sexual misconduct.

The realization of just how deeply rooted these practices were in the standard operating policies of the Church as a whole grew out of three events in my life, all of which came together to point to the same obvious conclusion.

The first event took place in the summer of that year. It was on Monday, June 12, at about 3:00 p.m., and my twin sister Kay and I were just returning home from a short vacation. We were driving out of San Francisco's International Airport onto the freeway when my right front tire blew out. Thank God we were in the far right lane so that I was able to pull over onto the shoulder, off the roadway. I was also grateful that I had a phone in the car so I could call AAA.

My sister, who is upbeat no matter what, said, "Jane, let's have a picnic. I still have a bagel and cheese left over from the lunch served on the plane." So there we sat munching on a bagel, waiting for a tow truck to arrive.

But the bagel didn't do much to relieve my frustration. The worst part was that we were headed to Mission San Jose, about thirty minutes down the road, to pick up my friend Sister Allyne Ayres, and it was already past the time we were due to pick her up. What would she be thinking as the minutes ticked by? Had she become anxious when we didn't arrive on time? With that, my car phone rang and it was Allyne. I explained to her that we were parked on the shoulder of the freeway waiting for a tow truck, and would get there as soon as we could.

At 3:30 p.m. we rejoiced as the tow truck pulled up next to us. The driver of the truck called out to me to move our car further off the highway, since I was almost in direct line with the oncoming cars. I pulled over, then got out to examine the damaged tire. I was horrified to see that the rubber all around the outer surface of the tire had peeled off like the skin of an orange! The gentleman from AAA explained that, judging from the way the rubber had simply peeled away, the blowout must have been due to a faulty tire. He advised me to take the tire back to Firestone and demand a replacement.

He proceeded to replace the shredded tire with my spare. Much to my dismay, I realized the spare tire was so small that, while it might make it to Mission San Jose, I knew it would never make the three- or four-hour drive back to Ukiah. By then it was 4:00 p.m. and I knew that I had to find a tire company before closing time. So after we picked up Allyne, I took her and Kay to a restaurant to wait while I went in search of a place where I could get a new tire. At that point I was beginning to have some very negative thoughts about the Firestone Corporation.

A few blocks from the restaurant I pulled into a gas station and was told that the nearest tire company was Pep-Boys, about four miles further down the highway. I prayed that they would have a replacement tire for my car. I arrived at the auto shop barely before closing time, hurried in and asked the attendant if they carried the size tire I needed. *Dear God*, I prayed, *please let them have the right tire!* The attendant went out to the shop to check and returned, saying, "Yes, ma'am, we do have the tire. One of our mechanics will be happy to install it for you."

I spent an exasperating fifteen minutes waiting while a very patient mechanic taught a young man how to change a tire! At this point, my feelings toward Firestone for selling me a defective tire had reached the point of anger.

With the new tire in place, I returned to the restaurant to pick up Kay and Allyne, and headed for Ukiah. But then I began to worry that one of the three remaining tires might also be faulty. I drove in the far right lane all the way home until I arrived in Ukiah at about 8:30 that night. Needless to say, I was most unhappy with Firestone!

A few months later I was visiting my niece and her family in Massachusetts, just outside of Boston, when I read in the headlines of the Boston paper that Firestone had been ordered by a judge in Oakland, California, to recall millions of tires. It was found that these tires were defective and had been responsible for one hundred deaths and over four hundred serious injuries. I thought to myself, thank God that Kay and I were not among those statistics!

From that day on I kept a file of news articles that dealt with the Fire-stone multinational corporation and the lawsuits that were being filed against it by individuals who had themselves been injured or had a family member killed because of the faulty tires. Something was germinating in my mind as I read the stories about how Firestone had covered up reports of the defective tire by settling out of court with the victims in exchange for their silence, while leaving the dangerous tires in circulation.

The second event occurred soon afterward, when I met with Don Hoard and his wife Marilyn on Thursday, November 12. Their son had been sexually abused by Father Gary Timmons of the Santa Rosa Diocese. The purpose of our meeting was twofold: Don wanted to thank me for going public with the story about Father Jorge Hume Salas, and I was gathering information in an effort to learn just how pervasive this problem was in our diocese. Don handed me a box filled with news articles, police reports and depositions. The box also contained two books on the sexual misconduct of priests and the lengths to which the bishops had gone to cover up the misconduct and prevent prosecution of the priests.

I spent the next four days poring over the contents of that box, stopping only to eat and sleep. There were documents dating back to February 1994, all dealing with the sexual wrongdoing of priests in the Santa Rosa Diocese and the Archdiocese of San Francisco. I was shocked and overwhelmed with the total disregard of any sense of morality on the part of bishops who for years had covered up these events.

Late one night as I read through all the materials Don had given me, it suddenly dawned on me that the Church had been operating according to the same principles I'd encountered in the Firestone Corporation. I realized that the Church was acting as though it must protect itself from criticism at all costs, even if it meant risking the lives of its supporters—even if it meant destroying the lives of children.

Like the CEOs of multinational corporations, the bishops—as heads of the diocesan corporations—put the corporations' reputations ahead of the well-being of the people who became victims of their actions. When both Firestone and the Church were sued by the people who had become their victims, those people were dealt with in the same way. The CEOs and the bishops covered up the actions for which they were being sued by settling out of court and rewarding the victims with monetary gain in exchange for their silence. The corporate heads would do whatever it took to protect the reputation of the corporation even if it meant using immoral and illegal means. Their concern was not for the innocent victims, but rather for the good of the corporation.

By this time, details of the Firestone tire problems were all over the newspapers and television news programs. It was obvious that the company had known they had some dangerous tires on the road, but people all over the country were filing lawsuits in the belief that the company had attempted to cover up the problem in an effort to save its reputation, and save millions of dollars as well. As a result, the suits claimed, hundreds of people were injured unnecessarily. I was horrified. If the claims were true, it meant that if the company had been responsible enough to recall every faulty tire as soon as it had reason to believe there was a problem, all those people who had put their faith in the integrity of the Firestone Corporation and the quality of its tires might never have been injured or, in some cases, killed.

I couldn't deny how much the plight of those injured people was like that of Don Hoard's son. How different the young man's life must have been before his trust in his parish priest was betrayed! The similarity between the actions of the Church and the actions of Firestone was clear. When a member of the clergy was found guilty of sexual and fiscal misconduct, the hierarchy of the Church settled out of court with the victims of that misconduct in exchange for their silence. The offending priests were allowed to continue to circulate in the Church—often sent to other parishes or even to another state or out of the country to avoid prosecution—just as the Firestone defective tires were allowed to circulate.

Think of all of the people who would not be dead or paralyzed for life if Firestone had recalled the tires when the first wave of accidents was reported. Think of all the young men who would not be forced to spend a lifetime recovering from the tragedy of sexual abuse if Bishop Mark Hurley had removed Gary Timmons from ministry after the first report of child abuse, rather than allowing him to continue to molest for more than twenty-five years.

When the Church as a corporation conducts its business based solely on secular values—when it puts monetary profit before compassion, when it covers up the abuses that would bring a bad name to the organization, and when it takes whatever means are necessary to ensure the preservation of the corporation even if that means acting illegally and immorally—it is betraying its role as the foundation of the spiritual lives of the people it was created to serve.

So how is it possible that God's Church can become an organization capable of harming the people who trust it so completely? The answer lies in the fact that the Church's structure as we know it, and the laws that govern its actions, were created not by God but by men. Given the human institutional structure of the Catholic Church, it is not difficult to see *why* the Church has much in common with the multinational corporations of today.

Donald Cozzens, in his book *The Changing Face of The Priesthood,* explains the human factor this way:

> The Church turns again and again to the Holy Spirit seeking strength and wisdom to remain faithful to its mission. Though grounded in the truth of the Spirit and guided by her wisdom, the Church as a human institution is subject to the patterns and dynamics identified by such social sciences as organizational development, systems analysis, and social psychology. To the extent that the Church ignores social patterns and organizational dynamics it risks losing sight of its pastoral mission and compromising its ecclesiastical integrity.[1]

Cozzens goes on to cite Harry Levinson's article in *American Psychologist,* "Why Behemoths Fell: Psychological Roots of Corporate Failure." Cozzens believes that Levinson's analysis of the failures of major corporations sheds light on the current crisis in the priesthood. The article suggests that the primary failure on the part of the corporations he examined rested with the executives of these companies, who were in denial. As Cozzens points out,

> their leadership became mired in "rigid corporate cultures and cumbersome hierarchies. The American corporate giants that failed to take seriously the data before them put their companies at risk and in doing so threatened the integrity of their corporate souls." In the eyes of many priests (as well as moderate, middle of the road

---

1.   Donald Cozzens, *The Changing Face of Priesthood.* (Collegeville, Minnesota: The Liturgical Press, 2000), p. 19.

Catholic Laity), Vatican officials and Church leaders appear to be
in denial of the Church's own data.[2]

What are these data? They appear in many forms, but clearly
include the prevalence of inappropriate sexual activity among priests,
the magnitude of the effects of this activity on the individuals against
whom it was perpetrated and on the Church community as a whole,
and the habitual efforts of the Church hierarchy to sweep the whole
dirty mess under the rug.

In a broader sense, I believe the Church's leaders are also in denial of
clear data pointing to the need for massive reform in every facet of its
operations, data that demonstrate that the people the Church was created to serve have evolved into a culture that is not recognized or
served by the manmade laws that the Church continues to uphold
while it ignores the realities of those people's lives. We can see evidence
of this denial in the refusal to recognize the need to ordain women
priests and married priests, the need to approve birth control methods
other than the rhythm method, even in the erroneous teachings on
homosexuality and the refusal to acknowledge that many of the clerics
are themselves homosexual. Given its adherence to "rigid corporate
cultures and cumbersome hierarchies," to use Levinson's phrase,[3] it is
easy to envision a failure of not only the Church's corporate soul,
but—just like Firestone Corporation—of its ability to ensure its own
survival at any cost.

The more we look the more we see how the Church functions like
an unethical multinational corporation. As a case in point, we see that
the Church has a glass ceiling that is thicker than that of any multinational corporation that I know of. Without exception, every "management" position, every position of power within the hierarchy of the
Church, is held by a man. That is a given, simply because each of those
positions is filled by a priest, and women are excluded from the priest-

2.   Ibid., p. 20.
3.   Ibid, p. 20.

hood. Women will never be allowed to hold positions of power in the Church as long as they are not allowed to be ordained as priests. Sexual discrimination doesn't get much more clear-cut than that.

If we're still not convinced that the Church operates with a corporate mentality, what better evidence can there be than the practice of charging for services rendered? About the time I was sorting through all the information about Firestone tires and Don Hoard's son, it also came to my attention that the Church provides services to people in order to make money. This policy might be fine for Firestone or McDonald's or the local bank, but the notion of charging a fee for serving the spiritual needs of parishioners is appalling!

The first shocking realization that this is the case came when one of our sisters who had been assigned to a parish in Pecos, New Mexico, told me that the first thing that caught her eye when she walked into the Church office was a sign in bold letters listing the cost for each of the services the priest performed. Those services included baptisms, weddings, funerals, Mass intentions,[4] and First Holy Communion. How could a church post a sign similar to one that you might see in a secular business?

The second time I was jolted into an awareness of this practice of charging for services was when I accompanied Sister Allyne as she made arrangements for her mother's funeral. The bill she received from the funeral home included a charge of fifty dollars for the priest. It so disturbed me that when I came home I went to our pastor and asked if he charged fifty dollars for a funeral Mass. He said the mortuaries typically include that sum for the priest's services. I was dumbstruck.

Every year my Order, the Sisters of the Presentation of the Blessed Virgin Mary, asks that the nuns in each parish arrange to have a Mass said for the intentions of our deceased sisters and benefactors. I was accustomed to making arrangements for the intentions, and paying the

---

4. Mass intentions are prayers offered by a priest at a designated Mass. Intentions are generally made at the request of someone in the parish, on behalf of a loved one.

parish secretary five dollars for each Mass. One day I went into the office to make the arrangements, and was told that the price had gone up to ten dollars for each intention. I was so upset about this that I left without paying the stipend. From that day on, I made my own intentions during whatever Mass I was attending.

It was also the practice in my parish to give an envelope to each parent of a child preparing for First Holy Communion, with the expectation that money would be donated to the Church on behalf of the child in honor of the occasion. As I became more aware of the implications of these practices, there was no way that I could continue passing out those envelopes. It made me feel that we were charging people for receiving a blessed sacrament.

When I reflected on all of these incidences of charging a fee for a service, I began to understand the outrage on the part of Martin Luther when he discovered that people received an "indulgence" when they contributed money to the fund for building Saint Peter's Church in Rome. An indulgence is a guarantee that the time spent in purgatory—a place of, you might say, "moderate" punishment somewhere between heaven and hell—would be reduced by whatever amount of time the Church granted. A Plenary Indulgence meant that if you died you would go straight to heaven. Talk about charging a fee for a service—!

Most big corporations exert a great deal of influence in all the places where they operate. The Catholic Church does, too. When Monsignor Patrick O'Shea of the Archdiocese of San Francisco was to be arrested for sexually abusing boys, the Chief of Police notified Archbishop Quinn, O'Shea's superior, prior to the arrest. This allowed time for the archbishop to prepare for the publicity that this arrest would receive. He placed O'Shea on administrative leave and sent him for treatment. The Chief of Police also told the two arresting officers to delete the priest's name from the report. O'Shea has since been arrested and is in jail awaiting trial, but thanks to its power and influence, the Church had the opportunity to mitigate damage to its public image.

Our parish school has a policy that if an eighth-grader receives a failing grade in any subject he or she cannot graduate. A few years ago when a bright but troubled eighth-grader received a failure notice, the principal notified the pastor that this boy would not graduate. The pastor told the administrator that this boy's grandparents had pledged a great deal of money to the Church building fund, and he did not want to risk their withdrawal of the money because their grandson didn't graduate. The boy graduated. I can't help but suspect that if the student had come from a poor family, the exception might not have been made for him.

As you have seen, the list of examples of this distorted sense of purpose on the part of Church officials goes on and on. There are countless examples within my own diocese and, I am sad to say, what goes on here is typical of practices all over the world. From the rampant sexual abuse we looked at in Chapter 2 to the fiscal improprieties at all levels of Church hierarchy, it's clear that there are policies and practices commonly in place that undermine everything the Church is expected to represent. And as we wonder how this can be, we find answers in the "corporate" cultural perspective that holds self-preservation and profit as the highest priority. It may be that some misguided clerics feel that perpetuating the life of the Church is a way of perpetuating the principles on which it was founded, but those poor souls have failed to notice that those principles have already been lost.

That is not to say that the principles of love and compassion that Jesus lived and taught, and on which the Church was originally founded, cannot be restored. On the contrary, just as I have seen the love and compassion in the eyes of members of my congregation—and, yes, in the hearts of the many dedicated and sincere priests all over the world—I believe that the Church can return to those principles and once again become a safe, sacred spiritual home.

Not power, not greed, but rebirth and renewal are the true teachings of the Church. Each of us has faltered, become confused, made poor choices—sometimes with devastating consequences. But just as every one of us can remember the love that lies deepest in our hearts, forgive ourselves and begin again with new hope, so the Church has an opportunity to return to its founding principles, turn these sad events into fodder for new growth, and see the flowering of a newer, brighter vision.

The hope for the Church lies in the people. As we continue our discussion we will explore how, by returning its power to those people, this multinational conglomerate can again become the caring, nurturing organization whose sole purpose is not profit, not self-preservation, but the spiritual growth of the people it serves.

4

Taught to Believe the Unbelievable

During the year or so after I went to the press with the story of priestly misconduct, my relationship to my faith changed dramatically. It seemed as though a series of revelations had come together to allow me to see the Church with new eyes. I had been forced to realize that the priests and bishops in my own parish and diocese were not the men I'd believed they were. I learned that misconduct and cover-ups could be found in parishes all over the world. And with my new, questioning perspective I understood for the first time that many common Church practices were designed for the preservation of the institution rather than for the benefit of the people it served. The very foundation of my belief had been shaken. It was inevitable that I would begin to question many of the teachings I had for so long accepted on blind faith.

My questioning eye turned to four basic areas: Church law, the sacraments, doctrine, and the legitimacy of the Church itself. In each of these areas I found places where some of the most fundamental teachings did not stand up to scrutiny. When I considered each area with an open heart I found places where mortal men had created rules, ideology, rituals and institutions, then passed them along as the teachings of Jesus Christ. In many cases I even found that that the implementation of these teachings was contrary to the true message of Jesus Christ.

It's not difficult to understand how I—like Catholics all over the world—was trained to accept these teachings without question. One of the principle ways the Church passes along its doctrine is through the

Baltimore Catechism, also known as *A Catechism of Christian Doctrine* (*CCD*). Like most children of my faith, I was introduced to the Catechism when I was in elementary school. It consists of 499 questions about the Church and the answers to those questions, which were to be memorized word for word. I remember being drilled in that doctrine as a daily part of my early schooling. If I, or any of my classmates, asked a question that was not covered in the Catechism, we were told that the answer was a mystery, and that we should accept that mystery on faith. I realize now that it was easy for the Church to appear wise and omniscient—why, this amazing book had the answer to every "legitimate" question. Then again, it's easy to have all the answers when you have all of the questions as well! It was simply a matter of controlling the minds of the faithful starting at a very early age, and training them to accept the Church's teachings on blind faith without question—and without scrutiny.

Apart from the catechism, we were made to learn the laws of the Church, which told us how to behave—what we should and should not do. To break any of those laws meant that you had committed a sin and needed to confess it to a priest to be forgiven. If you died without confessing a mortal sin, we were taught, you would go to hell for all of eternity—even if you were just a child.

Given the seriousness of the consequences of breaking these laws, it's rather startling to realize that most of them have nothing at all to do with the teachings of Jesus Christ. Most of them do have a stern "do not" associated with them. They include:

- Do not eat meat on Friday.

- Do not miss Mass on Sunday

- Do not eat or drink anything after midnight if you want to receive Communion the next morning.

- Do not let your teeth touch the Eucharistic host that the priest places on your tongue.

- Do not go into a church that is not Catholic.

- Girls, do not go into the church without a covering on your head.

- Do not do servile work on Sunday.

- Do not practice birth control.

The list goes on and on. Oddly enough, there is no law that says you have to feed the hungry or give drink to the thirsty, welcome a stranger or clothe the naked, visit the sick or imprisoned or forgive those who bring you harm. And yet, it is these actions that Christ himself—with His words and His deeds—taught us to value.

While Church law remains fuzzy in these areas, it is very clear when it comes to the more menial rules and regulations. Enforcing them is strictly a matter of black and white—there are no shades of gray, and no room for negotiation. My sister sadly tells the story of the morning that her two newly ordained sons, John and Kelly, were going to serve their first Mass. Kay rose early that morning and, in her excitement, forgot about her fast and took a drink of water. According to Church law, that meant she should not receive Communion on that day. When she arrived at the church she went directly to the sacristy and asked the priest there for permission to receive the Eucharist anyway. To her dismay, he told her, "Absolutely not, Kay. It would be a mortal sin!" As a result, my sister missed out on the chance to fully participate in that memorable moment in her sons' lives.

As I look back over my many years of teaching, I realize that I must have instinctively sensed the fallacy in these laws long ago. While I never questioned them consciously, there were many times when I knew in my heart that enforcing them was simply not the right thing to do. One bright Sunday morning when I was teaching at St. Mary Magdalene parish in Los Angeles, I was lining up a group of children for their procession into church on their First Communion day when one of the boys came up to me and said, "Sister, I forgot and took a drink of water."

I thought for a moment, then replied, "James, you know that you drank water, I know that you drank water and so does Jesus know that you drank water. But Jesus would not want you to be deprived of receiving your First Holy Communion when you and your parents and other members of your family have waited so long for this day. You are to stay in line and receive Communion. No one else has to know that you broke your fast."

The Church also has many laws regarding marriage. One such law states that if you are married in the Church and later divorce your spouse, then marry again without an official annulment, you may not receive any sacrament, including Communion. This, too, proved to be a law that I intuitively knew was contrary to the way we are meant to celebrate our faith.

When I came to Ukiah in 1973, I made it a habit to attend the 9:00 a.m. Mass. There was a couple who also attended that service every Sunday, and always sat in the same pew near the back of the church. It struck me as odd that they never went to Communion. After several months I approached them after Mass one morning and said, "I would like to ask you a question, but please—if you think it's none of my business, please tell me so."

They exchanged a glance, and then the woman replied, "What is the question, Sister?"

I said, "I noticed that you attend Mass every Sunday but never go up to Communion. I've been wondering why."

"Sister, my husband was married at the age of eighteen in the Catholic Church, and he and his wife got divorced a few years later. We were taught that if you married in the Church and then divorced and remarried, you could not receive Communion."

"How long have you been married?" I asked.

The wife answered, "For seventeen years."

I hesitated a moment, and then asked if they would do me a favor.

"Of course, Sister."

"Would you join me next Sunday and go to Communion?"

They looked at each other, then looked back at me. The woman thanked me for the invitation, but gave no definite answer whether or not they would in fact join me. We said our good-byes, and I was left to wonder what they would decide.

The next Sunday I saw the two of them take their usual place at the back of the church, and said a silent prayer that they would receive Communion. When the time came I went up to the altar to receive the Eucharist. When I returned to my pew, I looked up and saw the couple standing in line waiting their turn to join the others of us in the sacrament. As they turned to go back to their seats, tears were streaming down their cheeks and a beautiful glow emanated from their faces. I don't believe I have ever witnessed a more peaceful joy than that displayed by those two on that Sunday morning.

On another occasion, a beautiful young Hispanic woman came to my office on a Saturday morning and asked if she could speak with me.

I responded, "Of course you may."

"Sister, I am going to be married tomorrow in the Church, and I want to receive Communion. But, Sister, I have committed a mortal sin, and I cannot bring myself to confess it to a priest." In a very timid voice, she told me what sin she had committed.

I told the young woman that our pastor was a very gentle and understanding priest, and assured her that he would hear her confession and forgive her. She agreed to see the priest, so I called him and explained the situation. He agreed to come right over. When he arrived, I left the two of them in my office, closed the door and waited outside. It couldn't have been more than three minutes before the pastor came out and told me that the woman could not bring herself to confess her sin.

I went back into the office and asked the bride-to-be to look into my eyes, which she did. I said to her, "Sylvia, your sin is forgiven. God wants you to receive Communion on your wedding day."

Again, I saw a woman filled with joy as she virtually danced out of my office.

One of the sure signs that you are either Irish or Catholic is a vigorous sense of guilt. I am both Irish *and* Catholic, so I began to feel guilty about my lack of enforcement of these Church laws. I asked myself, "Jane, what authority do you have to reconcile people to God when they have disobeyed the laws of the Church?"

My immediate response was, "Because Jesus would have done the same."

Still, the question haunted me. Then one spring, my close friend Sister Allyne Ayres, O.P., invited me to go with her to Whitethorn, a Trappist monastery set deep in the redwoods of northern California. Allyne wanted to go to Mass at the monastery, and then to lunch at the Benbow Inn Restaurant, an historical landmark not far away. I gladly agreed to go with her.

We arrived in time to meet the Whitethorn nuns before Mass. We also met Father Roger, a Trappist monk who lived on the premises. I was struck by the man's gentleness, and by the spark of sincerity I saw in his eyes. That, and his slightly disheveled appearance, gave me the sense that he was a priest who was more committed to truth than to convention.

During the Mass I suddenly had the urge to go to confession. In preceding years I had not felt the need to confess my sins directly to a priest. At the same time, I had more and more frequently found myself in situations like those with Sylvia and James, in which I was encouraging people to violate Church law in the interest of practicing their faith with an open heart. I was troubled by my actions, and felt some conflict about whether I was really doing the right thing. I longed for the comfort of receiving absolution from a priest who really knew what I had been up to.

When the service was over I detained Roger and asked if he would hear my confession. He said, "Follow me down to my living quarters." With that, he got on his bike and pedaled down the hill to a building that had all the appearances of a motel. His two rooms were located at the end of the one-story complex.

I knocked on the door and heard the firm response, "Come in, Sister."

I opened the door into a room lined with bookcases, and with stacks of papers and more books piled on every surface. The sweet aroma of tobacco emanated from Father Roger's pipe.

With one swift sweep, Roger cleared the books from the chair that faced him. He invited me to sit down, and came to the point immediately, asking, "Sister, do you want me to hear your confession?"

I timidly responded, "Yes, Father. I have not gone to confession for several years, and I need to confess that I have been bending the rules. I have told people to go to Communion even though they have been divorced and remarried, because I felt it was more significant that they had been together for years and had been faithfully attending Mass. I have done this with more than one couple.

"I have also told a woman that her sin was forgiven when she could not bring herself to confess it to a priest."

As I continued my confession, Father Roger kept his eyes on me. He puffed steadily on his pipe, filling the room with the relaxing scent of the smoke. I felt the reassuring presence of a man that I believed was very close to God.

When I concluded my confession, Roger spoke those comforting words, "Your sins are forgiven. Go in peace."

I breathed a deep sigh as I felt a weight lifted from my shoulders.

He went on, "For your Penance, you are to continue to do what you are doing, freeing people to receive Communion."

When I rose to go, Roger placed his hand on my arm, looked me in the eye and said a quiet, "Thank you, Sister."

I left that smoke-filled room with the same feelings I had when I left the dark box of the confessional on the day of my first Confession. A voice inside of me said, "Rejoice, Jane, for your sins are forgiven. Know that if you die, you will go straight to heaven!"

A lot has happened since those days when I believed the laws of the Church were the laws of God, and breaking them might mean an eternity in hell. Once I began to see that much of what I had been taught about the Church was not what it seemed to be, I started to reexamine the whole system of rules I had been expected to uphold. More recently, in my questioning state of mind, I reached a point when I had to ask myself, "Jane, how can you believe that God would send someone, even a child, to hell just because they broke their fast and went to Communion anyway, or missed Mass on Sunday or ate meat on Friday—and did not confess their transgression to a priest?"

As the veil of blind acceptance was lifted from my eyes I began to see that those manmade laws, created by the mortal men who make up the hierarchy of the Church, do not have the power to define who God will and will not allow into heaven. They are guidelines established by human beings for the purpose of controlling the behavior of the faithful. What more powerful incentive for compliance could those human beings have chosen than to claim that breaking their laws would mean an eternity in hell? Powerful as that incentive is, it's sad to realize that those laws bear little resemblance to the fundamental guidelines of love and compassion given to us by Jesus Christ.

As this new insight became clear to me, I began to recognize that I had been responding to a voice of truth in my own heart all along. It occurred to me that Jesus clearly did not allow such arbitrary laws to govern His behavior or that of His disciples. Matthew's gospel says that Jesus allowed them to pick corn and eat it on the Sabbath, even though Jewish law at the time forbade it.

In another passage we are told that the Pharisees and scribes came to Jesus and said, "Why do your disciples break away from the tradition of the elders? They do not wash their hands when they eat food."

In response, Jesus said,

You hypocrites! It was you Isaiah meant when he so rightly prophesied:

This people honors me only with lip service,

While their hearts are far from me.

The worship they offer me is worthless;

The doctrines they teach are only human regulations.[1]

This whole system of creating "human regulations" that carry an eternal sentence for those who break them is just one of the ways in which Church authorities claim sole access to the voice of God. We are told that the pope is God's representative here on earth, with the "infallible" power to hear His voice. We are told that we need priests to act as intermediaries when we wish to worship or receive the sacraments. The hierarchical structure of the Church strives to strip us of our ability to hear the voice of God within our own hearts—except, of course, when what we hear is acceptable to the men in charge. When Church leaders claim the ability to enact laws that define who gets into heaven and who does not, it undermines a most fundamental element of faith for the rest of us—that is, the opportunity to know and trust God's guidance as He speaks to each one of us in the quiet depths of our being.

Once I realized that the laws of the Church are manmade laws that are not irrefutable, as I had been led to believe, I turned my questions to other teachings. It wasn't long before I began to wonder about the origin of the sacraments. Contrary to what I was taught, I no longer believe that Jesus instituted the sacraments—at least not the sacraments as we know them today. I believe the sacraments practiced and taught by the Church today, with all their attendant rules and regulations, were instituted by men.

The sacrament of the Eucharist is a good example. When Jesus shared bread and wine at the Last Supper, He asked His followers to "do this in memory of Me." As Catholics, we now commemorate this when we receive Holy Communion. But Jesus did not say that this sacred sharing should be done only in the presence of a priest, as the Church tells us, or only if communicants had consumed no water since the previous midnight. He did not say that people who had been divorced should not be allowed to participate, or those who had mar-

---

1.   Matthew 15:8-9.

ried outside the Catholic Church. Those regulations were added centuries later by mortal men who occupied positions within the hierarchy of the Church. By adding these—and many more—rules to the sharing of the bread and wine, officials have forgotten the spirit with which Jesus enacted this event, that all should come together in remembrance of Him and His message of love and acceptance.

Consider also the sacrament of Reconciliation, or Confession. Jesus tells us that all who come to God with an open heart in repentance will be forgiven their sins. He never said that God will only forgive us if we recite our sins to a priest, or if we say four Hail Marys and three Our Fathers as penance. Those practices were instituted by officials of the Church. But how ridiculous that is! Are we really to believe that God would deny forgiveness to someone who spoke directly to Him with a sincere heart? Here are these priests who are molesting children, forgiving each other their sins and then going out and doing it again—and we are expected to believe that we must go to one of these men, rather than speaking directly to God, if we are to be forgiven? No, I cannot accept that as a sacrament that Jesus would have instituted. Reconciliation as He offered it, with His words and with the offering of His death on the cross, is based on a blessing that takes place within the heart, between an individual and God.

A sacrament is a blessed moment in which we receive the grace of God. The ability to participate should not be based on whether or not an individual has abided by a series of rules and regulations, or on whether a priest is present. A sacrament is available to anyone who wishes to participate—sinner or saint, pope or layman, Catholic or not. Jesus welcomed everyone, and shared his message with all who wished to hear it. Who are we to do it any differently?

After much soul searching, I have come to realize that there are three fundamental doctrines of the Church that I no longer believe—two, because I feel that they give false messages regarding human sexuality as God's gift to us; the third, because I feel it places too much significance on the body of Christ, while it's in His spirit that we find our greatest healing.

First, the doctrine of the Immaculate Conception teaches that Mary, the mother of Jesus, was conceived without Original Sin. That suggests that she was in some way superior to all other women, since they were presumably conceived *with* that innate flaw. This doctrine is questionable because the basic concept of Original Sin has changed. We no longer teach that babies are conceived and born with that blight on their souls, but rather that they are born into a world that admits to sin. It follows that we no longer baptize babies to have Original Sin washed away. Instead, we believe that all children are born as God's children, and baptize them only to initiate them into a believing community. With the doctrine of Original Sin invalidated, the Immaculate Conception, one might say, applies not only to Mary but to all women—in fact, to men, as well.

Second, the doctrine of the Incarnation teaches us that Mary conceived Jesus by the Holy Spirit rather than by intercourse with Joseph. And yet, we have been told that Jesus was human in every way. Historical records certainly support this teaching. We know that He lived in a human body and even died a terrible death by crucifixion. Given those facts, why would God make an exception regarding how Jesus was conceived? Why would God provide humankind with the beautiful and intimate way man and woman have to love and support one another and bring new life into this world, and then make an exception for how the Son of God would be brought into the world?

My only response to those questions is this: The Catholic Church has a hang-up when it comes to sex. The message I get when told of the virgin birth of Christ is that there must be something shameful about the way most of us are conceived.

I remember the day I entered the convent. I left my family in the convent parlor and was ushered up to my cell—most of us would call it a bedroom—to change into my postulant dress and veil. When I entered my room I noticed two pictures on the wall. One was the picture of a beautiful young woman. It was Mary, mother of Jesus. The other picture was of an old, white-haired man. That was Joseph. The implication seemed to be that Mary would never have conceived a child by this old man.

Years later I read a book called *A Woman Wrapped in Silence.* I can still see the book's vivid illustration of Joseph on the night Jesus was born. The artist pictured Joseph as a strong, muscular man clutching the wooden beam that supported the stable roof, looking down at Mary and the infant. The inscription under the image left an indelible mark on my memory. It said of Joseph, "And he was the first to see her thus in all the world."

That author's interpretation notwithstanding, the Church has yet to develop a theology of human sexuality that is deep, uplifting and joyous. The doctrine of the Incarnation serves only to perpetuate a teaching that I believe to be false, in an effort to cast a specter of shame on one of the most meaningful of human experiences.

Finally, I take issue with the Church's teaching on the Resurrection of Christ. The standard doctrine holds that we have evidence that Jesus in fact rose from the dead, because his tomb was found empty. However, I agree with Edward Schillebeeckx's argument, as stated in his book *Jesus,*[2] that the proof of the Resurrection is not in the empty tomb—anyone could have stolen the body. The proof that Jesus lived after his crucifixion lies in what happened to his followers, in their conversion. After Jesus was killed, they were hiding behind barred doors, in fear for their lives because of their well-known association with him. Suddenly, two days later, they opened the windows and unbarred the doors. They began teaching His message openly to all who would listen, and even spoke out against those who had killed Jesus. It's clear that his followers were suddenly imbued with His spirit. That, I believe, is the more meaningful evidence that Jesus lived again, and still does today.

---

2.   Schillebeeckx, Edward, O.P. *Jesus* (Seabury Press, Crossroad, 1979).

Once it became clear to me that many of the Church's laws force people to live outside their faith rather than guide them toward it, that most of the sacraments were not instituted by Jesus but by men who came along centuries later, and that some of the fundamental doctrines of Catholic theology are invalid, I could no longer avoid looking with new eyes at the Church itself. Given all I had come to see about the way our Catholic Church is structured, the way it's governed and the teachings it offers, I can only conclude that the institution as we know it today is unlike anything Jesus envisioned for us. This church was created by men, for men. Women have no place in its leadership or its governance. Community has no role in guiding its future or selecting its spiritual leaders. The patriarchal, hierarchical structure that has appropriated Christ's name to serve its own end is crumbling under the weight of self-serving misconduct and deceit.

That the structure is crumbling does not disturb me. I do not believe we need a priest, a bishop or even a pope to save us. Jesus Christ has already done that. The image I cling to is one of the legendary bird, the phoenix, who after six hundred years rose up out of its ashes and soared once again in freedom and new life.

Members of the Church, people like you and like me, our brothers and our sisters, are beginning to realize their own priesthood—a priesthood that allows us to come together and break bread and share the cup...and know that Jesus is present. Among that priesthood the only laws that matter, the only doctrines that must be passed down, are those that are based on Jesus' most fundamental teaching: Simply love one another.

5

Homosexuality: A Biological Reality

Dallas, Texas: *Parked just outside the youth center of the Cathedral of Hope, the nation's largest gay church, is a white RV emblazoned with the legend "Jesus is Lord of all." For gay and lesbian Catholics, that simple statement is at the heart of the sexual abuse crisis in the church. Many are convinced that a witch hunt is underway—that gays are being blamed for the continuing avalanche of pedophilia complaints against Catholic priests.*[1]

Never before in the history of the church have revelations regarding the sexual misconduct of priests, bishops and cardinals been made public as they have been since stories of Bishop Ziemann and others began to emerge early in 2000, and the avalanche of accusations, criminal charges and lawsuits swept the country in 2002. Unfortunately, a number of the Church's most influential leaders have blamed homosexual orientation for the misbehavior of priests, and for pedophilic activities in particular.

In the midst of the furor, according to an article in *USA Today*, Archbishop Julian Herranz, who is the president of the Pontifical Council for the Interpretation of Legislative Texts and one of the most powerful men in the Vatican, reflected the views of other Vatican offi-

---

1. Marco R. della Cava, "Gays tell bishops: Don't blame us. Sex scandal heightens fears of persecution," *USA Today*, 12 June 2002.

cials who have linked sexual abuse with homosexuality when he "described pedophilia as a 'concrete form of homosexuality.'"[2] Psychiatrist and papal spokesman Dr. Joaquin Navarro-Valls has suggested eliminating homosexuals from the priesthood as a solution to the problem[3] and, according to the *New York Times*, declared, "People with [homosexual] inclinations just cannot be ordained."[4]

The truth is that experts who study sexual abuse make it clear that "homosexuals are no more likely than heterosexuals to be pedophiles,"[5] but statements like those of Herranz and Navarro-Valls reflect an inclination among many Church officials to blame the current crisis on homosexuality rather than consider the possibility that flaws within the institution of the Church itself may be fostering the problem. (See Chapter 6, "Uprooting the Roots of Priesthood.")

The Catholic Church's condemnation of homosexuality is not new. For centuries scholars and clergy have pointed to ancient Biblical passages as justification for claiming that relations between same-sex couples are evil. The story of the destruction of the city of Sodom is one example. As told in Genesis, Chapter 19, God destroyed the city after a mob threatened harm to visitors who were staying in the home of Lot. Like most of the Old Testament, the story was originally written in ancient Hebrew, and scholars don't always agree on the exact translation of the original text. But most everyone accepts the idea that the townspeople intended to rape the male visitors. Assuming that the mob was made up mostly of men, the rape would be considered a homosexual act and, according to some, that makes it so evil as to inspire God's wrath.

However, there are several problems with this interpretation. First, we might wonder if the intent to rape by itself would not invoke retri-

---

2.   Ibid.
3.   Ibid.
4.   Laurie Goodstein, "Scandals in the Church: The Sexuality Issue; Homosexuality in Priesthood Is Under Increasing Scrutiny," *New York Times*, 29 April 2002.
5.   Ibid.

bution from God, regardless of the sex of the perpetrators or their victims. Second, depending on which translation you read, it's possible that the mob also included women. If that's the case the group's intentions may have had less to do with homosexual acts than with doing violence and humiliating the visitors. That seems much more likely to have incurred the wrath of God, especially when you consider the culture in which the story took place. At that time there were very strict laws that required hospitality and protection be provided for all guests. Not to do so was unthinkable in that society, and it's reasonable to assume that breaking the law would have been grounds for retribution from God. In any case, while mass rape is unacceptable in most any culture, it has little to do with a loving homosexual relationship. It's difficult to rely on that story as a clear indication that God would disapprove the latter.[6]

I also find it interesting that, as the story goes on, Lot offered his virgin daughters to the townspeople in an effort to satisfy their demands while protecting the strangers. But Lot was saved from the fate of his fellow townsmen when the city was destroyed. God apparently did not see fit to punish him for his willingness to feed his own children to the lustful mob. If we take these passages literally, as some theologians say we should, what lesson should we learn about acceptable behavior from that part of the story?

Another biblical passage often cited is Leviticus, Chapter 18, which states, "Thou shalt not lie with mankind as with womankind: it is abomination."[7] On the surface it seems that this might be a fairly straightforward condemnation of homosexuality. But, again, if we look at the culture in which the story was written, it turns out that the meaning may have more to do with preserving the status of men than with making a judgment about sexual orientation. In ancient Hebrew culture, the status of women was similar to that of slaves and children. They were seen as property, while men were believed to be a manifesta-

---

6.   www.ReligiousTolerance.org/hom_bibg.htm.
7.   Leviticus 18:22.

tion of the image of God. Hebrew law, at the time, required that the superior status of men be preserved, even in their sexual relationship with their wives. The law is so strict on this point that men were even forbidden from having sexual relations with their wives in any but a dominant posture, with the woman taking a submissive posture.

Let's read that passage from Leviticus again, with that old law in mind: "Thou shalt not lie with mankind as with womankind: it is abomination." If two men were to have sexual relations, one of them would have to assume the submissive posture that was legally assigned to women. This by itself would have been a violation of the law and, therefore, "an abomination." This interpretation is also supported by the fact that many scholars believe the Hebrew word used in the original text would more accurately be translated "ritually unclean," rather than "abomination."[8]

Still, while many of the cultural laws and traditions of ancient Hebrew society have been cast aside, the Church's warnings against homosexual activity continue. The Vatican has been very definitive and clear in its condemnation of homosexuality. In 1986, Cardinal Joseph Ratzinger, who holds the most powerful position in the Church next to the Pope, wrote a "Letter to the Bishops of the Catholic Church on the Pastoral Care of Homosexual Persons." In it, he states that even if a person is celibate, homosexual orientation itself is a "strong tendency...toward an intrinsic moral evil." He goes on to say that "the inclination itself must be seen as an objective disorder," and that "special concern...should be directed toward those who have *this condition*."[9] (Italics added.) Not only does he cast a dark shadow on the moral fiber of homosexuals, but by calling same-sex orientation a "condition" Ratzinger suggests it is an illness that can and should be cured—a notion that is refuted by homosexuals and psychologists alike.

---

8.   www.ReligiousTolerance.org/hom_bibh.htm
9.   Cardinal Joseph Ratzinger, "Letter to the Bishops of the Catholic Church on the Pastoral Care of Homosexual Persons," 1986.

More recently, in July of 1999, Cardinal Ratzinger went a step further when he ordered Sister Jeannine Gramick and Father Robert Nugent to cease ministering to homosexuals. In 1971 the two had founded the unofficial Catholic organization they called Dignity, to minister to the needs of gays and lesbians. Many of the people they served were priests, brothers or nuns. For nearly thirty years Gramick and Nugent traveled the nation giving workshops and retreats for Catholic homosexuals. Although the two were committed members of the Church, in all those years they never suggested in any way that gays and lesbians were disordered individuals because of their sexual orientation. It was for this reason that Ratzinger demanded that they cease their ministry.

David O'Reilly reported on Ratzinger's action in Santa Rosa's *Press Democrat* on November 11, 2000. The article stated,

> After a decade-long investigation, the Vatican ordered Gramick and Nugent to discontinue their ministry. Rome…concluded that in their effort to be compassionate, [the two] had failed to remind listeners of the Church's teachings that all voluntary homosexual acts are an "intrinsic moral evil and gravely disordered."[10]

O'Reilly went on to explain that if Gramick and Nugent did not cease to minister to gays and lesbians, they were to be expelled from their Religious Congregation.

In spite of official pressure, Sister Gramick refused to be silenced or to cease her ministry to homosexuals. As a result she was expelled from her Congregation after forty years of service. Father Nugent, however, accepted the Vatican's order and ceased to minister to homosexuals. He felt that he could do more for homosexuals if he remained in his Religious Order and continued to work from within the Church.

---

10.   David O'Reilly, "Silenced Catholic Ministers React," *Santa Rosa (California) Press Democrat*, 11 November 2002.

Like Jeannine Gramick and Robert Nugent, many within the Catholic Church and beyond neither blame homosexuality for the current crisis in the Church nor condemn same-sex orientation as evil. In an article titled "Catholic Homophobia," human rights and sexual freedom activist Peter Tatchell speaks out against the blatantly anti-homosexual statements made by Cardinal Ratzinger. According to Tatchell,

> Ratzinger...deserves to be ousted because he is arguably the most homophobic of all Vatican leaders, being responsible for two of the most virulently antigay declarations ever made by the Catholic leadership.[11]

A position paper on the "Catholic Church Clergy Pedophilia Crisis" was recently released by the Northern California chapter of Call to Action (NCCTA), an organization of clergy and lay people dedicated to peace, justice, love and reform in the Church and society. The document points out that the Vatican's attempt to blame pedophilia on homosexuality is "some combination of maliciousness and ignorance. Homosexuality is completely unrelated to pedophilia. The Vatican seems to have no understanding of human sexuality."[12]

I, too, have felt compelled to speak out against the severe position taken by Church officials. I was so outraged to read that Cardinal Ratzinger had ordered Gramick and Nugent to cease their ministry to homosexuals that I wrote to the Cardinal directly, and asked him to account for what looks to me like a double standard with regard to homosexuality. How could he take action against these two compassionate ministers, and then allow Bishop Ziemann to continue his duties after acknowledging his own sexual activity?

In my first letter I asked the Cardinal, "Why is Bishop Patrick Ziemann still in active ministry in Arizona since Ziemann admitted pub-

---

11. http://www.outrage.org.uk/catholic.htm.
12. http://home.earthlink.net/~nccta/Pedophilia.htm.

licly that he had engaged in consensual sex with Father Jorge Hume Salas?" Referring to the Cardinal's 1986 Letter to the Bishops, I went on to say, "Cardinal, how could you, a human, fallible man, call any-one's actions 'intrinsically evil'? Nowhere in Scripture do we find Jesus condemning any actions on the part of individuals as gravely disor-dered or intrinsically evil."

Ratzinger had his personal secretary, Monsignor Josef Clemens, write a letter of response to my inquiry. The first sentence of the letter read, "His Eminence Joseph Cardinal Ratzinger has asked me to respond to your recent letter asking for a clarification concerning the Church's teaching on Homosexuality." He referred me to paragraph 2357 of the *New Catholic Catechism of the Catholic Church*, which explains that "homosexual acts are intrinsically disordered, and not the people who suffer from these tendencies. However, there is noth-ing—neither a person's good intentions nor any circumstances—that can morally justify engaging in homosexual acts."[13]

In the first place, the *New Catholic Catechism* was written by Church officials much like Ratzinger and Clemens, centuries after Jesus taught his message of compassion. Furthermore, as I explained to Ratzinger in a second letter, I was not asking for a clarification of the Church's teaching on homosexuality, but rather why Bishop Patrick Ziemann was still in active ministry as a priest and a bishop when he had con-fessed that he had a consensual sexual relationship with Father Jorge Hume Salas, while others were ostracized simply for ministering to homosexuals.

After a few weeks I realized that I would not get an answer to my second letter to the Cardinal, so I sent a third letter. My opening com-ment was, "Cardinal, you were so prompt in answering my first letter that I was convinced that you did not receive my second letter." For his convenience, I enclosed copies of my first and second letters. I shared with the Cardinal that I was writing a book, and that I didn't think he

---

13. Catholic Church, *The New Catechism of the Catholic Church* (Liguori Publica-
     tions, 1994), paragraph 2357.

would like to read in it that he had not responded to my letter. I sent the letter on February 14, 2001, and received a letter back from the Cardinal on March 12, 2001. I was beginning to feel as if Ratzinger and I were becoming pen pals!

Once again, His Eminence had his personal secretary respond to my inquiry. Clemens stated in the letter, "In answer to your request for information about the present pastoral ministry of the former bishop of Santa Rosa; unfortunately Cardinal Ratzinger has no knowledge of this matter. May I suggest that you direct your inquiry to the Congregation for Bishops, which would be the competent Dicaster."

What puzzled me was that in the Cardinal's first letter, he asked me to pray for the people who have been scandalized by the shameful situation in the Santa Rosa Diocese. That made it clear that Cardinal Ratzinger must know enough about those events to know that Ziemann is a homosexual. So given Ratzinger's condemnation of homosexuals, I still wondered how he could permit Ziemann to continue to minister as a priest. Again, this speaks to me of a double standard.

Sadly, Cardinal Ratzinger and his colleagues do not stand alone in their condemnation of homosexuality. The problem is not unique to the Catholic Church; it affects our entire society, and only recently has it come under serious scrutiny. In 1972 psychotherapist George Weinberg, Ph.D., coined the word "homophobia" to identify "a clear-cut but prevalent form of phobia [that previously had] not been defined as such by the experts because the sufferer's viewpoint jibes with most experts' opinions that homosexuals are disturbed."[14] Weinberg cited the need to shed new light on the issue of homophobia, noting that

> Volumes have been written—by psychologists, sexologists, anthropologists, sociologists, and physiologists—on homosexuality, its origins and its development. This is because in most western civili-

---

14.   George Weinberg, *Society and the Healthy Homosexual* (Garden City, New York: Doubleday, 1972), page 4.

zations, homosexuality is itself considered a problem; our unwarranted distress is not classified as a problem because it is still a majority point of view. Homophobia is still part of the conventional American attitude.[15]

Even today, one of the tragedies of homophobia in our society and in the Church is that individuals often feel they must remain silent about their homosexuality. While few of us participate in the physical violence often associated with anti-gay attitudes, it's probably true that many of us have some degree of homophobia within ourselves due to the cultural norms that surround us, and that helps perpetuate the problem. That reality came home to me in a conversation with a friend who is a lesbian. She shared with me that she had been in a relationship with a man for fourteen years. She said, "Sister Jane, I took an oath to myself that the bottom line regarding my sexuality would be to live with a man." However, in time she had to acknowledge that she found herself more attracted to women than to men.

As she began to realize that she was sexually drawn to women, she finally had an affair with a woman. Still, she believed that she would never be accepted if she acknowledged her sexual orientation as a lesbian, so she kept the affair a secret. Thankfully, she is now in a significant relationship with a woman who has lifted my friend's fear of not being acceptable.

Her story is powerful in that it illustrates just how pervasive our society's denial of homosexuality is. In my friend's case, as in many others, it caused her to be reluctant to admit her true feelings even to herself. Fortunately, with healing comes self-acceptance. Not long ago my nephew Sam, who is gay, told me, "Aunt Jane, when I was a teenager, I would have given a million dollars for a wand that would rid me of my homosexuality, because I thought that others would not accept me. Today I would not *accept* a million dollars to rid me of my homosexuality!"

---

15. Ibid.

Without a doubt, my relationship to Sam, as well as to his friends, led me to believe that homosexuality is a biological reality rather than a matter of the will. I remember vividly the day that my sister Kay called to let me know that Sam, her son, told her he was gay. She said that he wanted to tell each family member himself, and asked me not to let on that I knew. From the beginning, Kay and her husband Jim had no problem with the fact that Sam was gay. Not only do they accept him as he is, but they welcome his partner Scott, as well as all of their friends who are openly gay, into their lives, their home and their hearts.

A bittersweet effect of the negative attitudes of most of society toward gays may be a special sort of bonding among members of the homosexual community, as is often the case with people who are fighting a common enemy. Sam once told me a poignant story about his friend George that revealed the commitment, compassion and loving friendship that allowed the young man to withstand a difficult period in his life.

I had met George on many occasions over the holidays at my sister's house. Sam would bring him home often, and he became a part of the family. I remember Kay telling me that the young man was a great chef, especially when it came to making his specialty, a delicious gravy. At Christmas there was always a stocking and presents for George. On one holiday Kay shared with me that he had given her a beautiful crystal bell to add to her collection. Kay's remark to me was, "Jane, he spent too much money for that bell!" I could tell she was very touched by his thoughtfulness.

I soon learned that the reason George shared our family holidays was because his own family had disowned him when they learned of his homosexuality. Even so, when George developed a blood disease that hospitalized him, there was never a moment when he was alone. His gay friends made certain that there would be someone by his bedside at all times.

The time came when the family had to be notified that George was dying. When they heard the news they descended on George's hospital room—not to console him, but to squabble over who would get which of his possessions. In life they had disowned him, in dying they declared ownership of his belongings!

It's sad to see how fear and a lack of understanding can lead a family to be so cruel to one of its members. In a sense, that behavior is a reflection of the way society in general treats homosexuals. It is sadder still that the Catholic Church at this point is *not* a source of education and healing on this matter for families or for society. With no basis in fact, the Vatican's condemnation of homosexuals is an indication that Church officials share in the homophobia, and in a fundamental ignorance of the current understanding of the psychology of homosexuality and of biblical references to homosexual behavior. As if this weren't bad enough, this anti-gay and -lesbian stance has taken on a new twist in the face of revelations about pedophilia among priests. Church officials have compounded their error by equating the criminal act of pedophiles with homosexuality, a connection that is simply not based in fact. It is well known that, sadly, heterosexuals are all too frequently found guilty of sexually molesting children. In the case of the Church, many of the priests who have been accused of molesting children are heterosexual. Still, for Church officials, sexual orientation has become the scapegoat of a problem for which no one knows the cause or the solution. To compound the crisis by equating the criminal acts of pedophiles with homosexuality among priests is itself an abomination.

For too long, officials of the Roman Catholic Church have been condemning homosexuals out of biblical misinterpretation and an ignorance of scientific evidence, just as they condemned Galileo, the sixteenth century physicist and astronomer who told us that the earth was not the center of the universe. In November 1992, after 359 years, the Church finally admitted it was wrong about Galileo. As Peter Tatchell asks, "How many centuries will it take before the Vatican acknowledges the equally historic wrong it has perpetrated against lesbians and gay men?"[16]

At this point in the history of the church, it is critical that we openly acknowledge homosexuality as a biological reality, and make it an act of love and healing to welcome all members of the Church into our community. To do so may also be essential to the survival of the Church and the priesthood, because so many of the Catholic clergy are gay. Father Donald Cozzens, in his book *The Changing Face of The Priesthood*, points out that an NBC report on celibacy stated that "anywhere from twenty-three percent to fifty-eight percent of the Catholic clergy have a homosexual orientation."[17] He goes on to cite A.W. Richard Sipe's estimate "that by 2010, if the present trend continues, the majority of the clergy will be homosexual."[18] There is no question that many homosexual priests are beautiful, compassionate, deeply spiritual men ministering to their communities with all the grace and wisdom that Jesus asks of them. To suggest that these men be removed from their ministries, or to refuse to accept other homosexuals into the priesthood, benefits no one.

Homosexuals should be allowed to serve in the priesthood just as heterosexuals are—not as a result of the kind of indoctrination that occurs in the seminary system, but as spiritual leaders chosen by a parish from among its lay members. That would assure that the person each community chooses to preside at the sacraments and to minister to the spiritual needs of parishioners has clearly proven that he or she meets all of the requirements for priesthood. The candidates for priesthood would be selected for their spiritual gifts and leadership abilities, regardless of whether they are homosexual or heterosexual, single or married.

---

16.   http://www.outrage.org.uk/catholic.htm.
17.   Donald B Cozzens, *The Changing Face of The Priesthood*. (Collegeville, Minnesota: The Liturgical Press, 2000), p. 21.
18.   Ibid, p. 21.

As long as the Church remains silent on the topic of gay priests (or, worse, heaps the blame for unrelated problems on their shoulders)—and refuses to open its doors without reservation to lay homosexuals—there can be no healing or restoration of trust in the integrity of the Church in the hearts of the faithful. Unless homosexuals are allowed to celebrate their commitment to each other in the sacrament of marriage, just as heterosexual couples do, the Catholic Church will continue to deny the basic teaching of Christ—that we should love one another. We must love homosexuals and welcome them into our communities of faith. Anything less is aborting Christ's message.

I believe that the only way to heal from the blame, the mistrust and the name-calling is to come to a place of truth, honesty and openness on the part of the Church and society regarding homosexuals, where we can recognize and celebrate the many gifts they have given to the world as artists, scientists and priests. Until all prejudice against gays and lesbians is done away with, there will remain a deep wound on the body of Christ and the body of society.

The whole topic of human sexuality and homosexuality must be placed in the context of truth. The reality of homosexuality is a given and we must see this given as a biological reality. Only when we develop a theology of reality that allows us to cease living in a world of absolutes will we be able to embrace the lives and the hearts of all the people, in a context of the all-inclusive love that Jesus taught us to share.

Recently, I had a long visit with my nephew Sam. He told me about his struggle, as a gay Catholic man, to find a place in the Church. His story makes me very, very proud of him, with his sensitivity and his wisdom. It also gives me hope for the Church. I can't say it better than he did, so I'll let him tell you about it himself. Here is what Sam has to say:

> I was raised in a Catholic home where we attended church every Sunday and every Holy Day of Obligation without fail. Each week

we would file in together and sit in the very front row. Every Wednesday afternoon I would go to Catechism to learn about my role in the Catholic Church. As a gay man, I have been confident in my relationship with God. My relationship with the Catholic Church, on the other hand, has been cloudier. It is uncomfortable in much the same way as attending a party to which you have been invited and then feeling like the host doesn't really want you there. Nonetheless, my experience has at times been profound.

While studying in Europe in my late teens, I had the opportunity to visit the Vatican on a trip to Rome. Its presence and majesty overwhelmed me. Although I had not been in several years, I was moved to receive Communion so I ventured in to Mass. My favorite part of the Mass comes right before Communion where you say, "Lord, I am not worthy to receive you, only say the Word and I shall be healed." This was my secret way each week of having God make it all right for me, an abomination, to receive the sacrament. It always made me feel like I was well in the eyes of God. I took comfort in the idea that none of us was worthy, but each of us was accepted.

Since one shouldn't receive Communion in a state of sin, I decided to confess mine. I began, as you always do, "Bless me Father for I have sinned. It has been several years since my last confession…." The priest interrupted me to ask why, and I was dumbfounded. There is an order to things in the Church that shouldn't be disturbed. Boosted by the thought that maybe there is room in the Church for change and growth, I told him. I confessed to him that I was gay. To use a popular church metaphor, I told him that I felt like the sheep that was cut from the herd and abandoned. We chatted for nearly an hour. He told me that we are all God's creations and that He makes no mistakes. He told me that Jesus taught us to love and be accepting, and not to judge and condemn. It was a warm and compassionate exchange that remains with me to this day. At the end of my confession I expected the usual four Hail Marys and three Our Fathers. To my surprise, the penance he gave me was to go out and contemplate my relationship with God and the Church and try to find a way to maintain it, to be patient with an organization that is very old and slow to change. I was moved and filled with a sense of belonging.

Buoyed by his fresh new approach to the confession, I felt that I might find a fresh new Church to be a part of. Sadly, that has not happened. So I maintain my devotion to God and remember my Catechism: It can only be a sin if you truly believe that what you have done is sinful and wrong. I am proud to be gay and I believe that homosexuality is not a sin, nor is it a choice. It is a gift from God that not everyone understands, and because they don't understand it—they fear it.

Maybe I was created by God to test the faith of those who might doubt God's infallibility. Imagine if Job, in a surge of arrogance, decided to judge and condemn God's choices. The story would have a very different ending. I can only hope that the Church will learn and grow and begin to embrace all of God's creatures. The Catholic Church's problems with child abuse have no more to do with homosexuality than the problems they are having with deception and theft. Power corrupts. It is into this corruption that the Catholic Church must look to find resolution. After all: None of us is worthy to receive Him, but if He should say the Word, we shall be healed.

—*Sam Hamann*

6

Uprooting the Roots of Priesthood

"They went as a body to the Temple every day but met in their houses for the breaking of bread; they shared their food gladly and generously; they praised God and were looked up to by everyone."

—*Acts 5:32-36*

"But you are a chosen race, a royal priesthood, a consecrated nation, a people set apart to sing the praises of God who called you out of darkness into His wonderful light."

—*1 Peter 2:9-10*

These passages tell us about the earliest Christian community as it was in Jesus' time and soon after, before the creation of the Church as an institution. They describe a body of people who prayed together as one, who broke bread together and gave lovingly to one another. It was a priesthood of the people, all sharing the light of God without concern for power, rank or gender. It is dramatically different from the Church as we know it today.

Most people believe—and many Church officials would like us to continue to believe—that Jesus ordained twelve male apostles as priests, that He ordered them to be celibate, and that *they alone*, along with the priests who would succeed them, were given the authority to administer the sacraments and to deliver God's message to all Christ's other followers. These are the beliefs that support the existence of the patriarchal, hierarchical Church we know today. But as the passages at the beginning of this chapter suggest, this is not what Jesus had in mind. And there is reason to believe these mistaken beliefs have contributed to the current cultural attitudes that enable the rampant misconduct and cover-up that we see in the Church today.

One of the most comforting memories of my childhood is a painting of the Last Supper that hung in the dining room of my parents' home. Most of us have seen one version or another of that painting, usually with Jesus seated at a long table, flanked by twelve men—presumably the twelve apostles—sharing the Jewish Passover meal the night before He died. That image is important to many Catholics because a number of the beliefs that Catholics hold dear have roots in the Last Supper.

One of those beliefs is that on that night, at that table, Jesus ordained the twelve apostles as priests. However, there is no evidence in Scripture to support the notion that Jesus ordained the apostles at all, let alone at the Last Supper. In fact, we find no mention that He was even preparing His apostles for priesthood. But if that's true, how did the practice of ordaining priests among Christ's followers get started?

To answer that question we can look at the culture in which Jesus and His disciples lived. Given that it was the patriarchal—both civil and religious—culture of the Roman Empire, it is not surprising to see that Christianity evolved into a male hierarchical structure that defined itself as the Church. Elaine Pagels, in her book, *The Gnostic Gospels*, pinpoints a clear example of the authoritarian views of the men who, less than one hundred years after the time of Christ, had taken it upon themselves to dictate how His Church should be run. Some time between the years 90 and 100 C.E., with a perspective that is far different from any attributed to Jesus in any of the Gospels, Pope Clement wrote a letter to the Corinthians regarding the dismissal of some powerful Church leaders. As Pagels tells us, Clement saw this as a rebellion and called for the restoration of those leaders stating that they were to be "feared, respected and obeyed."[1] Pagels explains his reasoning:

> Clement argues that God, the God of Israel, alone rules all things: He is the lord and master whom all must obey; He is the judge who lays down the law, punishing rebels and rewarding the obedient. But how is God's rule actually administered? Here Clement's theology becomes practical: God, he says, delegates his "authority of reign" to "rulers and leaders on earth." Who are these designated rulers? Clement answers that they are bishops, priests and deacons. Whoever refuses to "bow the neck" and obey the church leaders is guilty of insubordination against the divine master himself.[2]

A decade later Ignatius, the bishop of Antioch in Syria, took this policy a step further. He pointed to the three-tiered hierarchical Church structure headed by a bishop, with priests and deacons in successive positions of authority, as representative of "a hierarchical order that mirrors the divine hierarchy in heaven."[3] Again, according to Pagels, Ignatius believed that

> as there is only one God in heaven...so there can only be one bishop in the Church. "One God, one bishop"—this became the orthodox slogan. Ignatius warns "the laity" to revere, honor and obey the bishop "as if he were God." For the bishop, standing at the pinnacle of the Church hierarchy, presides "in the place of God." Who, then, stands below God? The divine council, Ignatius replies. And as God rules over that council in heaven, so the bishop on earth rules over a council of priests. The heavenly divine council, in turn, stands above the apostles; so, on earth, the priests rule over the deacons—and all three of these rule over "the laity."[4]

---

1.   Elaine Pagels, *The Gnostic Gospels*.(Random House, Vintage Books, 1979), p. 34.
2.   Ibid.
3.   Ibid., p. 35.
4.   Ibid.

I find this concept of a hierarchical male structure that establishes all the power and authority of the Church in the hands of bishops, priests and deacons completely out of sync with Jesus' teachings. In John's gospel we see Jesus washing of the feet of His disciples, demonstrating how they must minister to others and to one another. Where is the hierarchy in that? It's clear that Jesus in no way intended for His closest followers to "bow the necks" of anyone.

It's also clear that He did not exclude women from among those who were closest to him. In fact, the notion that the twelve men we've come to know as His apostles—the same twelve men all of us have seen depicted in images of the Last Supper—were the only people in Jesus' inner circle of followers is a fallacy that, once again, grew out of the patriarchal culture of the Roman Empire in which Jesus lived.

Over and over again in the Scriptures we see Jesus breaking with the traditions of His day to treat women with the same regard He showed men. In John 4:25-26 we read that Jesus spoke to the woman at the well, and even disclosed to her that He was the Messiah. In that place and at that time, it would have been unheard of for a Jewish man to speak to a woman in public. To discuss religious matters with her, even to a minimal extent, would have been considered heresy.

In Acts of the Apostles we read that, after Jesus was crucified and ascended into heaven, those who were closest to Him went back to the upper room where they were staying. The apostles "joined in continuous prayer, together with several women including Mary the mother of Jesus."[5] In other words, when His most intimate, dedicated circle of followers gathered at a crucial time in their spiritual and personal lives, women were clearly among them.

These passages show us that from the start Jesus broke the barrier that excluded women from the teachings of God, and that—based on the culture in which He lived—would have otherwise excluded women from His own inner circle. Still, the official Church is light-years away from acknowledging the equality of women among its ranks. As we

---

5.   Acts of the Apostles 1:14.

have noticed, there is no more effective "glass ceiling" than that of the Catholic Church—in fact, there is not a single woman in a position of authority within the organization. Those positions are held by the pope, of course, as the highest authority, followed by cardinals and bishops, all of whom are chosen from among the priests. By excluding women from the priesthood the Church automatically bars them from being bishops, cardinals or—dare we think it!—a pope. Even deacons, the lay officials who often play a role in governing their individual parishes, are always men.

Just as the male hierarchy is an artifact that was imposed on the Church after Jesus died, so was the notion of celibacy among clergy. Nowhere in the Gospels do we find Jesus talking about the preeminence of celibacy over marriage. We know that the apostle Peter was married, since Jesus cured his mother-in-law, and there's no indication that Jesus objected to the marriage. Even into the first three centuries of the Church, there was no concern as to whether priests married or remained celibate.

The celibacy of priests was first decreed as clerical law in Spain, at the Council of Elvira in 305 C.E., when "it required 'bishops, priests, and all those who serve at the altar to live, even if already married, in continence.'"[6] I ask, how could a Council so dismiss the women involved who loved their husbands, and tell them that they could no longer be married? Once again, the answer lies in the culture in which the decree was made—a patriarchal culture that put little stock in what women thought.

Although this ruling was not supported by any of Jesus' teachings, officials throughout the centuries have pointed to Paul's first letter to the Corinthians as foundation for the requirement of celibacy. In that letter, he states,

---

6. Gordon Thomas, *Desire and Denial: Celibacy and the Church* (Boston-Toronto: Little, Brown and Company, 1986), p. 9.

> An unmarried man can devote himself to the Lord's affairs, all he
> need worry about is pleasing the Lord; but a married man has to
> bother about the world's affairs and devote himself to pleasing his
> wife: he is torn two ways.[7]

However, Paul prefaces that statement with the following: "About
remaining celibate, I have no direction from the Lord but give my own
opinion."[8] This is a classic example of the opinion of one man, in this
case Paul, passed down by modern day Church officials as though it
were the Word of God.

The requirement of celibacy has certainly contributed to the dramatic decline in the number of priests serving the Church today. Gordon Thomas, in his book *Desire And Denial,* refers to Paul's widely
misunderstood letter to the Corinthians in an exploration of the
impact of celibacy on the Church:

> When the Apostle Paul announced that to the Christians in the
> promiscuous city of Corinth, he unwittingly sowed the seed for an
> unprecedented crisis that today permeates the Roman Catholic
> Church. Beneath the panoply of the papacy, behind the wealth,
> power and influence of the Holy See [Vatican], is a profound strug-
> gle, one that is of crucial concern to its million and a half priests
> and nuns, its 810 million members, and to many beyond its fold.
> At stake is the future direction of a still powerful, dynamic, yet
> deeply perturbed and confused institution.[9]

The Church is now feeling the devastating effects of a crisis that first
began to appear in the 1960s when a series of events converged to
shake the foundation of the Church's religious orders. Vatican II
brought about many changes in Church law and ritual that helped to
make ancient traditions more meaningful in the context of modern day

---

7.   1 Corinthians 25:32-34.
8.   1 Corinthians 7:25-27.
9.   Gordon Thomas, *Desire and Denial: Celibacy and the Church,* (Boston-Toronto:
     Little, Brown and Company, 1986), p. 3.

reality. One of the most obvious of those changes was that the Mass, traditionally said in Latin—which, of course, few twentieth-century Catholics understood—was finally offered in English. In other efforts to bring rituals into the hands of the people, the Eucharist was administered by lay ministers and penance was offered as a communal celebration.

But perhaps the most wide-reaching impact of Vatican II was from the unprecedented free rein given to theologians. Much of the censorship that had silenced the more evolutionary thinkers was lifted, spawning a flood of writings about—among other things—sexuality among priests and nuns. All of this occurred in the context of the cultural upheaval of that decade, whose hallmarks were peace, love and sexual freedom. Suddenly the Church began to see a grand exodus among priests and nuns, along with a huge drop in the number of people entering seminaries and convents. In 1947, when I entered the convent, there were thirty to forty novices and postulants studying at our Mother House at any given time. Now, our order feels fortunate to have one or two women enter each year.

Nationally the statistics are devastating. Studies indicate that in 1965 there were 49,000 seminarians in the U.S., but by 1985 the number dropped by 75 percent to less than 12,000. During the same twenty-year period, the number of seminaries went from 183 to only about 30.[10] As Mr. Thomas puts it, "For every young man who wishes to enter Holy Orders [Priesthood], another has applied to leave."[11] What is the cause of this dramatic decline? According to a "poll taken in 1983, 94 percent of priests and nuns surveyed said an inability to live within the vows of celibacy…was their reason for leaving."[12]

The Church today takes its view of celibacy and the role of women to a point where it is not only hypocritical, but where women are devalued more than ever. I am convinced that the Vatican has no prob-

---

10. Ibid. p. 11-12.
11. Ibid. p. 4.
12. Ibid. p. 11.

lem with a priest having an affair, as long as he does not marry the woman. Several years ago, in my own parish, a former priest confided to me that when he had asked to be laicized so that he could marry the woman he loved, the bishop's response was, "Don't marry her! If you marry her you can't continue to minister. Why don't you just continue your affair with her?" Apparently the priest had a different sense of honor than did his superior. He left the ministry, married, came back to Ukiah with his wife and went to work as a counselor.

The notion of male priests holding positions of authority over other followers of Christ actually undermines people's ability to worship. When, at the Council of Trent in 1545, the Church passed a law that declared only priests were allowed to administer the sacraments,[13] it interfered with everyone else's right to speak directly with God and, specifically, to remember the covenant of forgiveness—the Eucharist—as Jesus instructed them to do.

The Eucharist is the most meaningful of sacraments for many Catholics. It's the one that they receive most frequently, often receiving Holy Communion at every Mass they attend, once or more each week. In addition, it represents a deeply intimate spiritual connection to Jesus, the sacrament in which we remember that He offered His life in love for each of us.

The meaning of Eucharist is one of those cherished beliefs that have their roots in the Last Supper. According to Scripture, that was the night Jesus shared bread and wine with His followers in what we now consider the first offering of this sacrament. As He passed the bread to the others He told them, "This is my body." Next, He shared a cup of wine with them, with the words, "This is my blood," and explained that He would give up His own body and blood in an eternal covenant of forgiveness. Finally, Jesus asked that this sacrament be repeated in remembrance of that covenant.[14] Two thousand years later, every Sun-

---

13.   Peter Stravinskas, *Our Sunday Visitor's Catholic Encyclopedia*, (Our Sunday Visitor, 1991), p. 940-941.

day at Mass, millions of Catholics remember that Last Supper when they receive the sacrament of the Eucharist—usually in the form of a wafer of bread administered by a priest.

However, Jesus never said, "Do this in memory of me, but only if a priest is around." In the early years of Christianity the community of believers would come together to share a meal, and then one of them would narrate what occurred on the night before Jesus died. The sacrament was shared by those who understood what it meant. They did not need an intermediary—a priest—to make it holy.

By the 1970s, in the aftermath of Vatican II, the Council of Trent edict that only priests could administer the Eucharist was, thankfully, repealed. Still, it was a struggle to get traditional clergy to release their hold on the sacrament. When I came to Ukiah in 1973 as the parish sister, I was part of a staff made up of five priests and myself. After the first month I mentioned at a staff meeting that I thought we should be preparing lay Eucharistic ministers.

The immediate reaction from the pastor was, "Well, if we allow lay people to pass out the Eucharist, then what will *we* do?"

I said, "Watch the ball game. Go and visit parishioners."

It was clear the priests felt their job security was being threatened. They would have none of it!

But many other parishes were beginning to use lay Eucharistic ministers. I continued to raise the idea whenever I saw an opportunity, and eventually circumstances made my position seem like the only sensible one. In 1977, after a series of staffing changes, we found ourselves down to only one priest. Our parish included three churches, the one in Ukiah and others in two nearby towns. One weekend Monsignor Mike Kenney from Santa Rosa came up to say Mass in an effort to help cover six Masses held at the three churches between Saturday evening and Sunday morning. This particular weekend we had an unusually large turnout for the 9:00 a.m. Sunday service. With no lay ministers, it took Monsignor Kenney twenty minutes to give out communion.

---

14. Matthew 26:26-29.

Before he left that Sunday he told the pastor, "I want, on my desk, the names of eight Eucharistic ministers by next week." Our pastor reluctantly complied with his request.

The notion that a priest is necessary to mediate between any one of us and our God has led to a practice that serves to reinforce the hierarchy of the Church. But when we take a closer look it becomes ludicrous, as we realize how it interferes with the ability of real life Catholics to practice their faith in the day-to-day realities of life. I remember a talk that Father Godfrey Diekmann, a missionary from Africa, gave at a conference in Washington, D.C., in 1983, that made this point very clear. He said that the missionary sister in the village he served came and asked him if he would go with her to the dwelling of a 100-year-old woman who wanted to go to confession and receive the sacrament of the sick. Father Diekmann got into the sister's jeep and off they went. When he entered the humble dwelling he saw the women lying on a mat in the far corner of the room. The Father approached her and tried as best he could to let her know that he was a priest. He heard her confession, though he had no idea what she was saying. He didn't know her language and she didn't know his. He completed the sacrament by anointing her in words she did not understand.

The whole room was silent when Father Diekmann asked us, "Who should have been anointing her and hearing her confession?" We all agreed when he said, "Yes—the nun who had ministered to her for years!"

Father Deikmann also told of a time when he was attending a funeral Mass for the pastor in that same village. When it came time for the homily the bishop, who was saying the Mass, turned and sat down facing the congregation. He said that he would remain sitting until a couple would come forward and agree to assume the role of priest.

An hour went by and finally two couples came forward. The bishop asked the women if they would support their husband if he were elected a priest and assumed the office of pastor to the people in the village. Both women agreed, and the bishop told them that he would return the following week and let them know which couple he had chosen.

That bishop clearly had a sense that the village would benefit from having members of its lay congregation minister as priests. This is an idea that makes sense for every parish. We must return to the practice of selecting individuals from among members of each local community to preside at the Eucharist and administer the other sacraments. These people could be single, married, female or homosexual. The choice would be made on the basis of each person's spiritual leadership and maturity. This, like all changes in the Church, must begin to take shape at the grass roots level.

I happen to believe in the priesthood of the laity, given my experiences with men standing at the altar who, the night before, had sexually abused a child. The most obvious benefit of this idea is that it would place well-respected members of the community in the role of spiritual leaders. It would place responsibility for the financial management of the parish in the hands of a committee of lay people who are skilled in such matters. And it would eliminate the current system of patriarchal authority that excludes women and demands celibacy. It would also honor the ability and the right of each and every individual to practice his or her faith and share the sacraments as Jesus taught us to do—without the need to wait for an ordained priest to appear.

Instituting a priesthood of the laity would also allow us to break free from the current system of seminary training that is causing many dedicated young people to turn away from priesthood, and undermining the mental health of those who attempt to endure it. Father James Kavanaugh, in his book *A Modern Priest Looks At His Outdated Church,* shares with the reader his "formation" in the seminary that he entered just out of high school:

> I was a seminarian and I cannot tell you what it meant. I cannot, with memory's help, tell you whether I was happy or sad, triumphant or troubled, longing to go on or afraid to give up. I only

know that I returned to the seminary year by year and ceased to be a man. I was a prophet, a hero, a soldier, a trained mind, a judge, a reformer, a contradiction, an ascetic, another Christ, an island, a crusader, but not a man. I could never again be ordinary, doubtful, carnal, or confused. I do not know what drove me, whether God, or man's respect, idealism, personal choice, or fear of hell. I only know that I struggled on and became a priest.... It was an education without sympathy, a training without recourse. I heard what I was supposed to hear, and said what the administration expected me to say. Rebels were weeded out. Only the strong and legal-minded, or the naïve and passive, could last. Creativity was discouraged unless it pursued the accepted patterns which cautious minds approved. "Heresy" was a word which ended every argument, and "the Church teaches" was a narrow outline of every debate. I was not educated, I was formed. I was not encouraged to think, but trained to defend. I was not asked to reflect, but to memorize.[15]

Is this really the way we want our spiritual leaders to be reared? And if this is the kind of mental manipulation that our seminarians endure, is it any wonder that the priesthood is beset with the moral uncertainty we see today?

We have arrived at a critical stage in which the Church has seen a rise in the number of priests who have left to marry, and a decrease in the number of young men entering the seminary. There would be no lack of priests if we could call forth married men, men with partners, women, and women with partners to be our priests. I believe that if we do not uproot the roots of priesthood and sow the seeds of a lay clergy, we are denying people their right to the Eucharist as Jesus intended it, as well as the opportunity to embrace the other sacraments as their own.

The rock of Peter is being chipped away, and the chips are building new ways of being a Church. It does not take a pope, a bishop, a cardi-

---

15.   Father James Kavanaugh. *A Modern Priest Looks at His Outdated Church*, 1967. p. 20-21.

nal or a priest to make Jesus present in our midst. We need only to gather in His name, break bread, share the cup and praise our Lord in prayer and in song. When we do, we are exercising the priesthood that was bestowed on us at baptism.

This does not mean that a priest, bishop or pope ordained and consecrated within the Catholic Church would be prevented from celebrating the Eucharist or ministering the sacraments for those who believe that priesthood is legitimate only for males who are celibate. However, the sacraments of the Catholic faith are not archaic events that occur only inside the four walls of the Church, at the hands of the few men designated as "holy" by officials in Rome. Those sacraments were created to embody the living, breathing faith of every individual who carries the love of God in his or her heart, and that dynamic quality must be restored. When Jesus shared bread and wine He pledged His body and blood in service to all men and women. The authenticity of our Eucharistic celebration today will be found in how we go forth and live justly, peacefully and with true love for all those less fortunate than ourselves. We are a Eucharistic people who make Jesus present wherever we go!

I believe that we are a Church of the people—people who are full of hope, who see our times offering us a great new way of being Church, just as Christ embraced His Jewish religion and expanded it to a new way of being holy by taking the message of the gospel to the poor and infirm, to the oppressed and to sinners.

Jesus said, "I have come to make you free. I have come so that you might have life, life more abundantly."[16] I believe that as we live and accept the truth of Christ, it makes us free to expand our faith to a practice that is true and alive in today's world. It has certainly made me free.

---

16. John 10:10.

We are a priestly people who bring the light, the truth, and the way to lift the burdens of the oppressed wherever they be. Our hallmark must be joy!

7

A New Vision of Hope for Society

Many years ago I read a story that made such an impression on me, to this day I remember it vividly. The story is about a young man named Gerard, who traveled to Paris every year for the annual conference held by his company, for which he was Chief Executive Officer of the United States division. There was a quaint family-owned inn on the outskirts of Paris where he always stayed when he was there. It was the inn where he and his French bride had spent their honeymoon during the war years of World War II.

On one visit, after checking in at the desk he took his bag up to the room and unpacked before heading down to the dining room for his evening meal. He ate a leisurely dinner, and then decided to take a walk before turning in for the night.

Exiting the lobby of the inn, he stepped down the damp stairs to the sidewalk below. The rains of the day had subsided and stars filled the clear blue skies. A bright moon shined down on Gerard as he strolled down the avenue. For no reason at all, he turned down an alley adjacent to the inn. Not more than a few feet into the darkness of the alley, he heard a cry. It was the cry of a baby.

Gerard looked down at the gutter and saw a small infant wrapped in soiled blankets, crying. The young man stooped down and picked up the infant, and enveloped the child in the strength and warmth of his arms. Holding the baby, he looked up to heaven and said, "God why don't you do something to help this baby?"

The voice of God responded, "I did. I created you."

In the wake of my going public with the story of Bishop Ziemann's cover-up of the activities of Jorge Hume Salas—with media people wanting to interview me and calls from individuals who wanted to tell me about their own experiences of sexual molestation by a priest—all the commotion began to take its toll. I could share the anguish of Frodo Baggins, the hairy-footed young hobbit in J.R.R. Tolkien's *The Lord of The Rings* who was charged with an overwhelming task: to journey to an evil land and cast the ring back into the fire of its origin. When Frodo felt he might crumble under the weight of his task, he asked, "Why do I have to be the bearer of the ring?"

One afternoon, smarting under the burden of having to deal with the press and individuals calling at all times of the day and night, I popped into St. Mary of the Angels school to retrieve my mail, and ran into Joanna Lopez. Joanna was a beautiful young Hispanic woman I had known since she was a child attending St. Mary's school and her mother Vera was the secretary. I said to her, "Joanna, why is God asking me to deal with Jorge?"

She looked into my eyes and said, "Sister Jane, God asked you because he knew you would do something about it."

The words that God said to Gerard rang in my ears; I could imagine him telling me, "I created you so that you could make a difference in your community."

I knew in that moment that being willing to make a difference in the lives of other people was the most important thing I could hold on to where my faith was concerned. In the preceding months I had seen the men I had been raised to trust and look to for guidance betray not only my own trust, but that of every parishioner—children and adults alike—in their diocese. I had come to understand that all those rules about eating meat on Friday or not drinking water before going to Communion have very little to do with what Jesus taught. But standing in the hallway, with Joanna looking up at me with her big honest eyes, I knew that what matters most when it comes to behaving like a Catholic is the way we care for one another, how we respond when we see someone in need. That's what our faith is really about. In the weeks and months that followed, I found a great deal of strength in the realization that the ability to respond to trouble in our own hearts and in our community with courage and with love is the best and truest way to live as Jesus would have wanted us to live, as individuals and as a Church.

When I looked around me I could see that many, many good people were doing just that. I had just moved into a house in a lovely neighborhood in Ukiah when I initiated my war on the weeds in the front yard. One summer afternoon a young woman crossed the street with a plate of homemade chocolate chip cookies still warm from the oven. She introduced herself.

"I'm Jeanne Nevills from across the street, and I wanted to welcome you to the neighborhood."

I introduced myself and we talked about her son Jordan, who was in junior high. Jeanne told me she had five other children who had already left the nest and married. She went on to say that she and her husband Gary saw more of the children now than they had when the youngsters were living at home. We chatted a while longer, and I thanked Jeanne for her thoughtfulness before she went on her way.

Days melted into weeks and months, and I became curious about the number of babies that appeared at the Nevills' home. Often I would see Jeanne or Gary carrying little ones into the house, or watch the two of them head out for a walk on a summer evening, each one pushing a stroller. My curiosity was satisfied one afternoon just before Thanksgiving when Jeanne and Gary brought over a tiny baby, just a few days old, to meet me. The infant had become a ward of the state because the mother was unable to take the baby home with her when she left the hospital.

Gary shared with me that he and Jeanne were foster parents. He explained that they had wanted to continue to raise children after their own were grown, but felt that they were too old to have more children themselves. They had considered adoption but decided to become foster parents instead, and open their hearts and home to infants that had become wards of the state after birth because the mother was unable to provide a safe home for the baby. Jeanne laughed when she told me that at times they'd had as many as three infants all under the age of one month, which meant they were fortunate if they could get as much as three hours of sleep at night!

The following January, for the thirtieth anniversary of their marriage, Gary made reservations for the two of them to go to Las Vegas. Everything was paid for in advance. However, the evening before they were to leave they received a call from the foster care agency, asking them to take in another toddler who was in need of a home.

Jeanne said to Gary, "Las Vegas will always be there, but this baby won't."

They canceled their trip.

One bright spring day just before Easter, Jeanne confided to me that she often wondered if they should have attended church services when the children were young. She went on to say, "Sister, we had six children and it just seemed there was no way to get all of them ready at the same time to attend church on Sunday morning." She was quick to add, "Of course, I believe in God, and I pray to God all the time."

My response was, "Jeanne, I know people who occupy the front pews in church each and every week, but could not hold a candle to the Christian way of your life." It was clear to me that God had created the Nevills to care for the little ones that so desperately needed a safe and loving home to go to.

Jeanne and Gary are rejoicing now because at last the father of a little boy named Shawn has relinquished his right of custody so that they can adopt him. The Nevills have had Shawn since he left the hospital just after his birth. From the beginning there was something very special about the bond that developed between this child and his kind foster mom and dad. Jeanne and Gary soon realized that this was a child that they wanted to be a part of their lives forever. After months of paperwork and prayers, they finally got word that the adoption had been approved.

When they got the good news, Jeanne brought her son over to see me and to say that they felt our prayers had been answered. Little Shawn is ten months old now, and has two loving parents along with plenty of uncles and aunts and cousins who make up his new family.

As for Gary and Jeanne, they continue to be the best of what our faith teaches us to be. They are doing the kinds of things that Jesus asked us to do, opening their hearts in love to those who are in need.

Sometimes it takes the good will of many people, working together, to make Jesus' message a reality. In the summer of 1983, a young man by the name of Martin Bradley asked a question that snowballed into a community effort that has since taken on a life of its own. Martin came into my office one afternoon with a binder tucked under his arm. He placed the binder on my desk and asked me, "Sister Jane, would you like to open a dining room to feed the poor and homeless of our community?"

Without hesitation I responded, "Yes. It has been a dream of mine for the past ten years, ever since I've lived in this area." Over and over again since I arrived in Ukiah, I had encountered the poor in our community, and I had made it a priority to visit them where they lived. The poverty was self-evident. I was always moved to see how they struggled to get by on meager wages or what little assistance was available to them. I found people making do with their families squeezed into tiny one-room apartments at the edge of town. Others lived in fragile trailers on the Indian rancherias. Still others were migrant workers, housed in makeshift dwellings on the ranches where they had come to harvest grapes or pears.

Martin opened the binder resting on my desk and showed me a picture of two buildings on Main Street that were vacant. The County Social Services had moved out when they secured another site. The

Main Street property was owned by a plastic surgeon who lived in Santa Rosa. He had put the buildings up for rent until he could find a buyer.

As we talked about the possibilities it became clear that Martin and I shared a vision of hope for the poor in our community. We decided at that moment that I would set about raising the money while he would negotiate terms to secure the buildings.

I can picture it as though it were yesterday when Martin, Debra Meek, Susan Crane, Ann Near, Ginny Lindstead, Mary Rice, the Anderson couple and I sat in the bare room of the larger building on Main Street. The Andersons had brought wooden folding chairs on which we sat and squinted to see the chart that Martin placed on a wall in front of us. Without electricity, it was hard to see. But our vision of hope, that no one would go hungry in our city, was becoming a reality.

Martin recorded on the chart paper what needed to be done before we could open our Community Dining Room doors. The tasks were written on the chart along with a list of who would do what to accomplish them. Martin offered to get volunteers to renovate the building into a dining room. Debra, Susan and Mary would create a plan for how we could get the food and beverage needed to feed the poor. Ginny would arrange for the use of the Methodist Church kitchen once a week to prepare the food, and recruit people from the church to serve the meals. I would secure the finances necessary to operate the project. We decided to base our operation on the Catholic Worker House, in that we planned to support ourselves on the generosity of people rather than rely on government funding.

On November 15, 1983, we opened our doors. It was hardly three months since Martin and I had decided we would open a dining room for the poor. Since then it has evolved to include a personal care and resource center, where people in need can shower and do their laundry, receive medical care and counseling, as well as a place to receive phone calls from family members and to facilitate job searches. It would take a book to tell all that we went through in establishing Plowshares Dining

Room and Personal Care Center. Suffice it to say that the vision became a reality because we believed that it could happen, and because a compassionate and dedicated group of people from all around the community joined together to care for those in need.

Every city has its homeless, and each community sooner or later faces the need to open a shelter to bring the homeless in out of the cold. But anyone who undertakes the job of founding a shelter is likely to meet with opposition from the neighbors. The problem is this: Everyone wants a shelter, but few are willing to put it in their own backyard.

In November 1999, concerned citizens were searching for a building that could house the homeless of Ukiah. Letters went out to every church asking if they would be willing to open their doors to the homeless. Mary Leittem Thomas, pastoral associate for St. Mary's Catholic Church in Ukiah, brought the letter of request to our staff meeting. She read the letter, and we as a staff discussed the possibility of opening our new parish hall to the homeless during the winter months.

The proposal was to open the shelter December 15 and close it on March 31. Mark Rohloff, the director of the Ford Street Project, which offered services and housing to individuals who wished to get off drugs and alcohol, had indicated that his organization would assume the responsibility of operating the homeless shelter. Not only would our parishioners be called on to volunteer their services but the community at large would be asked to volunteer as well. It was to be a community project.

What made this decision painful was the fact that for more than thirty years the parishioners of St. Mary's had dreamed of having a parish hall where they could gather for coffee and donuts after the Sunday Mass, as well as a place for meetings, adult education programs, a youth group drop-in center and many other activities. After years of praying and planning and fundraising and building, the new hall had finally been completed that summer. To say, "Yes," to the request to provide space for a shelter meant that the hall and the adjacent youth room would be tied up for the winter months.

As a staff, we weighed the pluses and the minuses of the proposal. The reality of housing the homeless would be in the spirit of Jesus' description of the Last Judgment where he says, "I was hungry and you gave me food; I was thirsty and you gave me drink; I was a stranger and you made me welcome."[1] As Christians, we knew we should heed the words of Jesus and open our hall to strangers, knowing that as we did we would be welcoming Jesus into our midst. Unanimously we agreed, and sent word to Mark Rohloff.

Next, we called a meeting so that the parishioners could hear from those who would oversee the shelter, and have an opportunity to express their concerns regarding the shelter. One concern that was raised by more than one person was a fear that the shelter would be too close to the elementary school. I reminded them that the Plowshares Community Dining Room and Personal Care Center, which had been providing meals and personal services to the homeless for more than sixteen years, were just as close to the elementary school, and I assured them there had never been a problem regarding the school in all that time.

At one point, a gentleman stood up and began to shout at Hans, our pastor, for making the decision to open the parish hall as a shelter. With that, I went up to the microphone and asked the gentleman to sit down and wait his turn to speak.

He responded, "I will not sit down."

I said, "Fine, remain standing but do not interrupt people who are speaking. You'll have to wait your turn to speak."

He turned and stormed out of the room.

I went on to say to the group, "On Christmas Eve we will be celebrating Mass in the church across the way. We'll hear the story of how Mary and Joseph found no room at the inn. For me, it would be very

---

1.   Matthew 25:35-39.

difficult to see the hall dark and empty that night, when it could be lighted and giving shelter to the homeless in our community as we celebrate the birth of Christ."

Father Hans made the final decision to proceed with the plan to open our hall to the homeless of Ukiah. At the close of the meeting a group of people remained to form a hospitality committee that would help to create community with our homeless. They didn't want people to just have a warm place to sleep, so they agreed to make sure that each evening at 6:00 p.m. when the shelter opened there would be people from the community at the door to welcome each guest.

On December 15 the doors to the shelter officially opened and the greeters welcomed the strangers. The parishioners not only welcomed their guests but had also prepared food, milk and coffee so that no one would go to bed hungry. A variety of games were put out in the shelter, and the guests and volunteers could be seen playing chess, checkers or card games together. The next morning at 6:00 a.m., the volunteers arrived to make breakfast for the guests before they had to vacate the shelter at 8:00 a.m.

And so it went, evening after evening, morning after morning on through the cold winter months. When the doors were closed on March 31, the guests and the volunteers were no longer strangers but friends. Tears flowed as they bade farewell to the guests with promises of keeping in touch. The shelter had become a way for people of all different churches and segments of society to come together and make a difference in the lives of homeless families and individuals.

I will never forget that Christmas Eve when our parish opened its heart and home to the less fortunate of our community. The Christmas evening Mass was at 5:15 p.m. I had just stepped inside the door of the church when I heard someone call my name, and I turned to look at the pew close to the door. Very much to my surprise, it was Rick, the director of the shelter.

He said, "Sister Jane, you didn't know that I was a Catholic did you?" Rick was a tall, well-built, persuasive man who only had to speak once if someone in the shelter was disruptive. I knew that he had gone out and bought presents for the children and teenage guests, as well as the adults. He'd wrapped each gift and given them out earlier that evening.

I answered, "No, Rick. I've never seen you come to Mass before."

He smiled and said, "It's been a long, long time. But when I saw St. Mary's Catholic Church open its doors to the homeless, I knew it was time I came back."

When I came out of Mass on that Christmas Eve, a woman came up to me and asked, "Sister Jane, would you come into the shelter and tell the children the story of the First Christmas? I think that some of them have never heard the story."

"Of course I will." With that I went into the hall, and found it packed with children and adults, all smiling and singing Christmas carols.

As they settled into a circle around me, I began the story with the words, "You are so special to Jesus, because he was homeless, too, when he was born." Every eye was on me and they hung onto every word as I described that first Christmas when the Son of God was born in Bethlehem.

I will never forget that very special Christmas Eve, when I had the opportunity to share the love of Christ with the homeless of our city.

The wonderful experience shared by everyone involved with the shelter at St. Mary's has inspired a new vision for finding ways to serve a much broader range of needs for the poor and homeless in our community. A committee has been created by people who envision a permanent shelter for the homeless that will accommodate both families and individuals, with space for their dogs. That first winter season, forty of the homeless people would not go into the shelter because they could not bring their dogs. The committee decided that when people who have so little are willing to care for an animal who has less, they should not be turned away. An architect has been hired to draw up plans for a new facility that would not only house a shelter, but also be the new site of the Plowshares Community Dining Room, along with the Personal Care Center. I have every hope that this wonderful new facility will be up and running before long.

Being a church has little to do with whether or not you eat meat on Friday, or whether or not a priest is present to lead people in prayer. Being a church means living the way Jesus taught us to live, and taking his teachings into consideration as we interact with one another each and every day. When love and compassion are behind the choices we make, when we take the time to care for those in need, we create Jesus' church with our actions and with the changes we create in our community. The only rules that matter are those that help us remember to love one another, as He taught us to do.

8

A Journey of Faith Concluded

Every story has its ending and so I bring my story to its conclusion, knowing that my journey of faith is not ended here but will continue for the rest of my life.

Many people have asked me, "Sister Jane, have you left the Catholic Church?"

My answer is an emphatic, "NO!" I was literally born into the Catholic Church and I remain a Catholic. For the last fifty-five years I have been a Catholic Religious of the Sisters of the Blessed Virgin Mary, and I continue as a Sister of that Order today.

As I look back on my journey, I am reminded of a book that I read over thirty years ago that explains my journey and how I have arrived at a point in my life where I am so free. The title sums up the message of my book, as a new vision of hope for the Church and society. *Hope For The Flowers* is a story about a tiny striped caterpillar who burst from the shelter which had been home for so long and dropped to earth to see a whole new way of being in the world—not as a caterpillar but as a butterfly who flew free of the cocoon that had encased her. As she gazed at the world with new eyes, she knew that cocoon would never encase her again.[1]

In my childhood I was wrapped in a cocoon of beliefs that I was taught to believe, and rules that I was taught to obey as though they had come from God when, in fact, they were created by men to control and manipulate the faithful. The butterfly within me began to flutter

---

1. Trina Paulus, *Hope For The Flowers* (New York: Newman Press, 1972).

as I tried for two years to have Jorge Hume Salas removed from priesthood and then learned that Bishop Patrick Ziemann not only covered up the sexual and fiscal misconduct of Jorge, but was himself involved in a sexual relationship with Jorge. That experience forced me to see the Church in a new way, with a more open mind. I began to question all the beliefs and rules I had accepted without question, and I set out to find answers that made sense. My truth no longer hangs on statements from the Church but rather on what I know to be true in my conscience and in my heart.

At the heart of all I went through is the marvelous revelation of a sense of freedom that I never had before. I had accepted the authority of the male hierarchical church, had accepted the teaching that the pope was infallible and that priests were other Christs—but all of that crumbled. Now I find myself free. At last I've come to experience the freedom that Jesus told us we would know if we lived the truth.

As I write this I am healing from three fractured ribs and carpal tunnel syndrome. With all of my pain I'm happier than I have ever been, because I'm free. I no longer live my life within a cocoon of the walls of the Church. I no longer allow human laws to bind me, nor do I allow someone else to determine who I'm going to be, what I am going to do, what I'm going to say or not say. I have reached a new level of maturity in which I am no longer looking for answers outside myself. My faith is of the Spirit, and the laws I obey are those that come from my heart.

Before the events of these past few years my life was controlled by the laws, rules and practices that had been handed to me by the institution of the Church. Now I am controlled by no one beyond my own conscience; I now live totally by the God within me. At last I understand that the only way people can find God is to search within themselves.

As I've come to rely on God's presence within my own heart, I've also discovered His presence in the whole of creation. And just as I no longer accept a hierarchy within the Catholic Church, I no longer see a hierarchy anywhere else in God's creation. A tree is no more valuable than flowers. Flowers are no more valuable than rocks. With God all things and persons are of equal value.

Why am I saying this, when ten years ago I was saying something else? Ten or even five years ago I could not say what I am saying today, or share what I have shared in this book. All of this has emerged because of the crisis—the crisis of Jorge Hume Salas and Patrick Ziemann, the sexual molestation in the Church, and my own crisis in the realization that so many of the things I had accepted on faith were not true. The journey through all those crises led me to the blessing of truth, and of a new way of seeing the world. I understand now that we must look beyond the scandal, look beyond the details that caused this pain, and see the crisis as a springboard, a chance to break out of the cocoon into free flight.

When faced with a difficult decision, I no longer ask myself, "What does the Church teach?" I look within my own heart, and from my own heart I come to decisions that I believe are more loving, forgiving and compassionate.

I fervently hope and pray that those who read this book will be freed from all of the constraints that hold them in a cocoon and, like the caterpillar, will shed the cocoon and fly free as a butterfly!

Epilogue

I pray that all who read this book will dare to envision a world and a Church…

- Where leaders take it upon themselves to see that people of all races, creeds and classes can succeed in acquiring those things that feed life and spirit, so that they have everything they need to become fully human.

- Where leaders are concerned for the safety of children, young adults, women—all those who might suffer at the hands of those who would take away the personal power of others.

- Where leaders will not tolerate sexual abuse of any kind.

- Where no one accepts the authority of another over the voice of God in his or her own heart and conscience.

- Where each Catholic parish and diocese can select its priests and bishop locally, from among its faith community.

- Where Catholic priests can choose a life partner and marry, whether they are heterosexual or homosexual.

- Where women of the Church can become priests and bishops so that the balance of power is shared by both men and women.

- Where lay people become responsible for the finances of their parish and diocese, so that the clergy can attend to the spiritual needs of their flock

- Where married couples can, without interference from the Church, determine how many children they can support.

- Where people gather together in Christ's name to break bread and share the cup in the sacrament of Eucharist—whether or not an ordained priest presides—in a way that enriches their worship and their relationship with God and with each other.

- Where the Church, in resonance with Pope John Paul II, reaches out to all churches and people of other beliefs.

- Where no one goes hungry or homeless.

- Where all may be gainfully employed.

- Where all members of the global community have the things they need to enable them to realize their human potential.

- Where women and men, homosexuals and heterosexuals are treated as equals.

- Where no one in the world is oppressed.

- Where the wall of discrimination is done away with so that people of other nations can, if they wish, come to America to better their lives.

- Where violence is never used to settle a disagreement.

- Where all arsenals are plowed under and all people live in peace and justice.

- Where the Catholic community joins hands with people of all races, creeds and social status to bring about the Kingdom of God on earth.

Now you have envisioned the Kingdom of God that Jesus tells us is within each of us. Let us now live that vision and bring about the Kingdom of God on earth.

Bibliography

Berry, Jason. *Lead Us Not Into Temptation: Catholic Priests and the Sexual Abuse of Children*. New York: Doubleday, 1992.

Boonprasat-Lewis, Nantawan, editor. *Revolution of Spirit: Ecumenical Theology in Global Context: Essays in Honor of Richard Shaull*. Grand Rapids, Michigan: William B. Eerdmans, 1998.

Catholic Church. *A Catechism of Christian Doctrine*. Revised edition of *The Baltimore Catechism No. 2*. Paterson, New Jersey: St. Anthony Guild Press, 1941.

Catholic Church. *Catechism of the Catholic Church*. Liguori, Missouri: Liguori Publications, 1994.

Catholic Church. *Code of Canon Law*. Washington, D.C.: Canon Law Society of America, 1983.

Catholic Church, National Conference of Catholic Bishops. *Economic Justice For All: Pastoral Letter on Catholic Social Teaching and the U.S. Economy*. Washington, D.C: U.S. Catholic Conference, 1986.

Catholic Church, Pope John Paul II. *Encyclical Letter of John Paul II on Social Concern*. Boston: St. Paul Books & Media, 1987.

Catholic Church, Pope Paul VI. *Encyclical Letter of His Holiness Pope Paul VI on the Development of Peoples*. New York: Paulist Press, 1967.

Catholic Church, Pope Paul VI. *Respect For Human Life*. Boston: Compiled by Daughters of St. Paul. Boston: St. Paul Editions, 1987.

Chittister, Joan, O.S.B. *Winds of Change: Women Challenge the Church*. Kansas City, Missouri: Sheed & Ward, 1986.

Congregation for the Doctrine of Faith. *On the Unicity and Salvific Universality of Jesus Christ and the Church*. Boston: Pauline Books and Media, 2000.

Cook, Bernard J. *Theology in an Age of Revolution*. Denville, New Jersey: Dimensions Books, 1963.

Cozzens, Donald B. *The Changing Face of Priesthood: A Reflection on the Priest's Crisis of Soul*. Collegeville, Minnesota: Liturgical Press, 2000.

Crosby, Michael H., O.F.M. *Spirituality of the Beatitudes: Matthew's Challenge for First World Christians*. Maryknoll, New York: Orbis Books, 1981.

Curran, Charles E.. *Transition and Tradition in Moral Theology*. Notre Dame, Indiana: University of Notre Dame Press, 1979.

Day, Dorothy. *The Long Loneliness: The Autobiography of Dorothy Day*. New York: Harper and Row, 1952.

Fox, Matthew. *Creation Spirituality: Liberating Gifts for the Peoples of the Earth*. San Francisco: Harper San Francisco, 1991.

Gorg, Manfred. *In Abraham's Bosom: Christianity Without the New Testament*. Translated by Linda M. Maloney. Collegeville, Minnesota: Liturgical Press, 1999.

Hamm, M. Dennis. *The Beatitudes in Context: What Luke and Matthew Meant*. Wilmington, Delaware: Michael Glazier, 1990.

Haughton, Rosemary. *The Passionate God*. New York: Paulist Press, 1981.

Investigative staff of the *Boston Globe*. *Betrayal: The Crisis in the Catholic Church*. Boston: Little, Brown and Company, 2002.

Jefferson, Thomas. *The Jefferson Bible: The Life and Morals of Jesus of Nazareth*. Boston: Beacon Press, 1989.

Johnson, Elizabeth A. *She Who Is: The Mystery of God in Feminist Theological Discourse*. New York: Crossroad, 1992.

Jordan, Mark D. *The Silence of Sodom: Homosexuality in Modern Catholicism*. Chicago: University of Chicago Press, 2000.

Kavanaugh, James. *A Modern Priest Looks At His Outdated Church*. N.p., 1967

Keane, Philip S., S.S. *Sexual Morality: A Catholic Perspective*. New York: Paulist Press, 1977.

Martin, Malachi. *Three Popes and the Cardinal*. New York: Farrar, Straus and Giroux, 1972.

Nolan, Albert. *Jesus Before Christianity*. Maryknoll, New York: Orbis Books, 1978.

Nouwen, Henri. *Intimacy: Pastoral Psychological Essays*. Notre Dame, Indiana: Fides Publishers, 1970.

O'Brien, David J., and Thomas A. Shannon. *Renewing the Earth: Catholic Documents on Peace, Justice, and Liberation*. Garden City, New York: Image Books, 1977.

Pieper, Jeanne. *The Catholic Woman: Difficult Choices in a Modern World*. Los Angeles: Lowell House; Chicago: Contemporary Books, 1993.

Quinn, John R. *The Reform of the Papacy: The Costly Call to Christian Unity*. New York: Crossroad Publishing, 1999.

Ratzinger, Joseph with Vittorio Messori. *The Ratzinger Report: An Exclusive Interview on the State of the Church*. Translated by Salvator Attanasio and Graham Harrison. San Francisco: Ignatius Press, 1985.

Redford, John, Rev. *What Is Catholicism?: Hard Questions—Straight Answers*. Huntington, Indiana: Our Sunday Visitor, 1997.

Rohr, Richard and Joseph Martos. *Why Be Catholic?: Understanding Our Experience and Tradition*. Cincinnati, Ohio: St. Anthony Messenger Press, 1989.

Rutter, Peter, M.D. *Sex in the Forbidden Zone: When Men in Power—Therapists, Doctors, Clergy, Teachers, and Others—Betray Women's Trust*. Los Angeles: J.P. Tarcher; New York: Distributed by St. Martin's Press, 1989.

Schiblin, Richard, C.S.S.R. *The Bible, the Church and Social Justice*. Liguori, Missouri: Liguori Publications, 1983.

Schillebeeckx, Edward, O.P. *Christ, the Sacrament of the Encounter With God*. Translated by Paul Barrett. English text rev. by Mark Schoof and Laurence Bright. Scheed and Ward, 1963.

———. *Church: The Human Story of God*. Translated by John Bowden. New York: Crossroad, 1990.

———. *Jesus: An Experiment in Christology*. Translated by Hubert Hoskins. New York: Crossroad, 1979

Segundo, Juan Luis, in collaboration with the staff of the Peter Faber Center in Montevideo, Uruguay. *The Community Called Church*. Translated by John Drury. Maryknoll, New York: Orbis Books, 1973.

Sipe, A.W. Richard. *Sex, Priests, and Power*. New York: Brunner/Mazel Publishers, 1995.

Stone, Merlin. *When God Was a Woman*. San Diego: Harcourt Brace Jovanovich, 1978.

Stravinskas, Peter M. J., editor. *Our Sunday Visitor's Catholic Encyclopedia*. Huntington, Indiana: Our Sunday Visitor, 1991.

Swidler, Leonard, and Herbert O'Brien, editors. *A Catholic Bill of Rights*. Kansas City, Missouri: Sheed and Ward, 1988.

Thomas, Gordon. *Desire and Denial: Celibacy and the Church*. Boston: Little, Brown, 1986.

Unsworth, Tim. *Catholics on the Edge*. New York: Crossroad Publishing, 1995.

Wallis, Jim. *The Call to Conversion*. San Francisco: Harper and Row, 1981.

Weinberg, George. *Society and the Healthy Homosexual*. Garden City, New York: Doubleday, 1973.

Wills, Gary. *Papal Sin: Structures of Deceit*. New York: Doubleday, 2000.

Winter, Miriam Therese. *Out of the Depths: The Story of Ludmila Javorova, Ordained Roman Catholic Priest*. New York: Crossroad, 2001.

Printed in the United States
1535500005B/300